Bend Without Breaking

How Struggles Build A Resilient Faith

MARY HUNT HAUSER

Bend Without Breaking

HOW STRUGGLES BUILD A RESILIENT FAITH

MARY HUNT HAUSER

Contents

To Charlie, my husband and best friend, who offers endless encouragement and insightful wit, and knows the stories that were left unwritten.

Preface

HOW TO USE THIS BOOK

I believe God led you to pick up this book for a reason. You are going through something right now, and you fear it may break you. But I want to assure you: God is with you in the storm. He will use these struggles to strengthen you.

Read each slowly and thoughtfully. Take your time. Stop to reflect on the verses I cite. Perhaps you'll want to look them up in your own Bible, consider their context, and pray through them.

At the end of each chapter, you'll find a list of the key takeaways. Maybe you'll pick one that resonates with you and write it down in your journal or on a note card to carry with you.

You'll also find one spiritual practice. Even if it's a practice that's new to you, I'd urge you to experiment with it. In my own life, spiritual practices have helped me to move their truth from my head to my heart. In this book, you'll learn the truth *about* God: how He helps us to live resilient lives. But in the practices, you'll experience the presence *of* God. You'll be equipped to live that resilient life. To bend without breaking.

CHAPTER 1
Getting Back Up

Resilience is not a trait that you're born with; it's a set of skills that can be learned.

—Dennis Charney and Steven Southwick[1]

MY HUSBAND and I sat in straight-back chairs nervously waiting for my surgeon. This was not a social call. He had just performed a biopsy on my left breast and as I sat there the tension was mounting. He would not have sent word to meet him in his office if all was well. In silence I counted the framed photos that lined his walls. Twenty-five. Each picture documented a fresh kill. Animals were hanging from a pole, on the ground or posed on a truck hood. The surgeon and his hunting buddies hunkered around each prize, triumphant, the battle behind them. A brown bear stretched horizontally in a glossy 8-by-11, my surgeon smiling proudly at his side. In the next photo, he leaned his bow onto an elk's impressive antlers. This procession continued: a four-point buck, an antelope, a water buffalo, a mountain lion and what was once a majestic Bighorn sheep. My surgeon posed alongside him, touting his tool of choice, a rifle mounted with a high-powered scope.

I swallowed the fear that tightened around my throat.

I tried to think that his hunting triumphs would be helpful to me. He liked winning. He would want my operation to be successful. He used his hands for precision and his eyes for exacting measurements in tracking an animal. There was no margin for errors. He wouldn't have made mistakes with my biopsy either. I followed the framed procession that continued around each wall. The surgeon positioned his tool of trade next to each conquest. They were somehow less the animal they had been because he was good at what he did. He was a professional, someone who knew what tools to use and how to use them. My meeting with him was one he had had with many other patients. I sat still, waiting for my turn.

The door creaked and he entered the office from behind us. Making his way to his desk, he sat down and transmitted that same triumphant smile. It quickly turned to a grimace as he opened my file onto his desktop. I was next.

"I don't have good news. It is breast cancer and because of the location, I am recommending a mastectomy."

I repeated his words to myself. I have cancer. I need to have a mastectomy. I have cancer...

"Don't worry," the hunter continued, "I am very certain we can get it all." He paused as though looking through the scope of his trusty rifle. He searched for our reaction.

"Do you have any questions?"

I turned toward my husband who looked much like I did. We were deer caught in the headlights. Was he repeating my diagnosis in his mind too?

"Anything?" I asked him. Silence.

"Not right now," I told the surgeon.

I couldn't think of anything to say. His words had caught me. I was 39 years old, and I needed a mastectomy. I blinked back tears, holding onto the silence as though my pause could put off what was coming.

The next day the questions would line up one after another. I would form one question about what caused breast cancer and end in research areas that were over my head. I would dig into treatment options and that would bring an overload of what if's, revealing a future that I didn't want to imagine. Questions would twist and convolute, then multiply with a certain frenetic energy about them, like a thundering herd of wild antelopes running from a hungry lion. How long has this been in my body? How fast will it grow? What if the cancer has metastasized? What if it wasn't found in time?

At night, my questions became a safari heading into a no-man's-land of shaming and blaming. What did I do to cause this? Will I have enough faith to fight it? Will I be unable to take care of my children? Will I ever sleep through the night again? Is this how I die?

The questions led to much-needed prayer and then professional counseling. I walked the neighborhood for hours, as though the next steps would conquer the doubts. I would sift through and rate which scriptures seemed best for breast cancer. I wondered if God would lead me to a silver bullet of verses that would slay this enemy. Each day and each question created more uncertainty, revealing a vast, unknown spiritual territory. Which step to take first? What to believe? Where do I go for help? Why was this happening?

It had all started right after my dad's death, when I felt the Lord leading me to seek Him via a 40-day fast. My father was my hero. He was my motivator and my confidant. Wise, gentle, and encouraging, he always had the words of hope I needed. Within the last two years, he had shrunk to half his size as he battled against lung cancer and then heart issues. In April he played Jesus in his church's Passion Play. By August he was gone.

The pain was palpable. Yet, my day-to-day life continued. We moved into a larger house; I finished finals and graduated from college. I processed the deep haze of confusion the books call denial in a Christian grief group. I found solace in the stories others shared as they navigated life with the shackles of grief weighing them down. I facilitated a small group of leaders for our church that was planning a church plant. I was trying to do life, but mostly just going through the motions.

One day while swimming laps on the last week of the fast, I felt a stab of pain in my chest. I thought I had pulled a muscle. I massaged the area around the pain and immediately felt a knot. What was that? I had lost so much body fat that what would have been hidden for much longer was now visible when I peered in the mirror. What followed the first surgeon's diagnosis were two two-week hospital stays, six months of chemotherapy, a chest infection, a blood clot, and anaphylactic reaction to contrast dye in a routine scan. Though I received intense prayer sessions, overwhelming support from friends, and pastoral counsel, I still felt that I had entered a parallel universe. I was healthy. I was thirty-nine. I was a believer, faithful, a lover of God. How was this happening? It was so foreign to what I knew and expected of life that I did not know how to make sense of it. This was not supposed to be my story.

What I didn't know then was that this was the first of five cancer diagnoses I would receive in my life. It would test the limits of my faith and build resilience. I also didn't know I would survive.

Have you felt that way too? Have you experienced a situation that was so overwhelming it created a version of reality that did not seem like your life? Did it seem as if there was no way to return to the way it was before? How do you find a way to get back to normal? How do you navigate the unknown territory of faith when everything seems to be falling apart, when there is no steady ground to walk on?

Learning to walk

Each of my children learned to walk. But did I "teach" them to do so? Of course I encouraged them, holding out my hands for them to toddle toward. But they learned this life skill by falling and getting back up, repeatedly. They really taught themselves to walk, with my encouragement. But the process taught them life lessons about resilience as well: when you fall, you get up and try again. By repeating this process, they learned that their consistent efforts would lead to mastering a skill. They would learn to walk.

We can determine to get back up after and even during hardships, difficulties, or trials. We tell ourselves what a toddler's parents tell them: "Great job! You've got this! Look at you go!" We don't think a

4

baby's first steps are flawed, even though they objectively are just that--unsteady and unreliable. We encourage their process. Over time, they walk with steady, strong legs.

Just like learning to walk or ride a bike, we learn to cultivate resilience when we struggle. We learn that the process of continuing through a difficult situation grows this intangible thing in us. Without the difficulties in life, we would all be on a beach in Fiji taking in the rays and never grow spiritually, change, or mature in character. In that sense, struggle is prerequisite for growing resilience. No one is born with it. But everyone develops it as we persevere despite the circumstances life brings our way.

Although your situation may be very different from mine, we all experience trouble, hardships and crises. Is grief over your divorce getting in the way of the decisions you need to make? Is your father's sudden heart attack resulting in overwhelming caregiving needs? Is the foster child who you thought was settling into your family not able to make it through a routine school day? These are circumstances that do not have quick fixes.

When one crisis happens and the previous one hasn't resolved, it can feel relentless. Finding your way can seem hopeless. When you feel lost and alone, the anxiety may overwhelm you. Even though what we face is vastly different, there are foundational supports that are the same for all of us. Truth is still the truth. God is still leading you in the way you should go. Especially in the middle of a crisis we need to be assured that we will be alright. God is present in the difficult circumstances with us, and we can trust Him.

His promise to be with us makes all the difference. His presence affirms our purpose as we navigate tough situations. Nothing is wasted in God's economy. He uses the problems we are faced with to strengthen our faith. To know that He has purpose in it, helps us to endure and persevere. He will make a way, a path, a method to move us forward.

Our daily choices affect whether we are leaning toward God or away from Him. Doing it our own way is one of those choices. If we see ourselves as the victim, the martyr, or the proud overcomer, we are choosing our ways instead of God's ways for our lives. Living life on our own, independent of His counsel and guidance, is easy; we just do what comes naturally. We can suck it back up and prove to ourselves, "I've got this!" We can fake our proud selves right into chronic fatigue, attempting to gloss over the impact of it all. When it all seems to be too much, we can push Him to the edges of our healing process, push Him outside of our grief or only allow Him in the margins of our search for answers. If that's your choice, He will allow you all the space you need. (*Selah*, pause and think about that.) We can do it all on our own. And that will seem to work for a while. But a place and time of reckoning comes.

We do have choices how we allow God into our crisis, into our impossible situations, and into our healing process. When I first heard the word cancer, I reeled from the emotional impact. I was shocked and silent, trying to find a safe place to process the emotions. But as time evolved, so did my feelings. Given friends, family, and God's encouragement, my emotions were no longer overwhelming my ability to think. Soon I was not overcome by the diagnosis, even though the facts had not changed. I was able to analyze surgical options, choose from the treatments offered, and gather supportive resources.

Through these pages I want to offer you choices. I want you to re-form a perspective about what may have seemed impossible in the past: you can come through incredible difficulty and bend without breaking. The choices offered are the how-to's of walking with God. They are small steps that interrupt the emotional implosion that can come when crisis strikes. They are supportive measures to take before clear solutions arise. They are ways to dialogue with ourselves and others to become more aware of our need to let go of expectations. They are steps to apply verses the Lord is using to instruct you. The goal in considering these options is to support your faith as crisis strikes. Letting go of God, who is our source of strength, will only bring additional pain to our suffering. Choosing to hold on to Him is an act of faithfulness; one we are willing to make.

You can make choices to build resilience in your life, even as you read through these chapters. Resilience will grow as you make changes and recover from stressful and traumatic experiences. Your ability to adapt, change and learn from your struggles will encourage you. The Lord will highlight truths you can apply because He is creating a pathway for your life to grow resiliency as you walk through current situations. Choosing to process emotions, apply spiritual truth, and receive His grace will support your physical, emotional, and spiritual health. Even in the middle of a crisis you can pause to hear God and become more aware of His presence. That choice can begin to ease the tension.

We can choose to remind ourselves that His mercy and grace are available in the middle of the crisis. His love and faithfulness are never ending. His power cannot be contained. These eternal qualities are offered to you. He will meet you right where you are today. Saying yes to Him is the best solution in navigating through adversity and seasons of hardship. He will bring you hope, a light to your path, and redemption that comes in ways you haven't seen. Easy? No! Doable? "All things are possible for those who believe." (Mark 9:23, ESV) You can build faith as you navigate through your current struggles. He is your answer for trauma, anxiety, and hardship. He is your hope. He will create in you a heart of resilience. He will build a more resilient faith through your current challenges.

Use the difficulties

I have lived through cancer five times. There was something unique and different about each situation. My first diagnosis came when my husband and I were raising four-year-old twins and a ten-year-old.

One afternoon after school, soon after the breast cancer diagnosis, my ten-year-old son and I were sitting at the table as he struggled with his math homework. He stopped maneuvering his pencil, looked at me with his big, brown eyes and asked an unpredictable question about why God allowed me to get cancer.

"You are God's friend. Why would He treat His friends this way?"

He waited for my response. His face told me of the fear he was holding in. I gulped.

God has mysteries that are sometimes too big to explain, especially before his tender mind could make sense of it. I took a deep breath as my faith helped me to form words that I could only somewhat understand.

"He will take care of us through this. He promises us that!" I could only give him what I had; a belief that despite the trauma of cancer, God was in control.

I would tell the twins about why I would be in the hospital, why I couldn't drive at times, and why people delivered food every week. I used a calm voice and assured them: I would be home soon, there would be changes in routines, but soon it would be behind us.

Cancer brought questions about my ability to endure. Every day the choice was the same: would I face the day's battle by leaning into God or away from Him? Would I allow Him into the pain, the mess, and the everyday ugly of it all? Some days there would be great spiritual surges. I would be on my knees on the kitchen floor and worship would consume me. He would illuminate scripture, and I felt confident and steady. But more often, I needed the life-giving fuel of His Word and His presence because the day could feel as dry as a desert. Those times were marked with monotonous, boring repetition of saying yes to God by writing Him letters in my journal and highlighting verses. It was as simple as offering Him space and time. It was when I did not shy away from Him that faith grew. It was when I reached out for Him that He showed me He was right there.

The truth is I'm still working on how and when to use the strategies in this book. Each challenge I deal with will require me to think through and pray about how to apply what I know in a different way. I must be open to using them with wisdom each time I face a crisis. For instance, I have learned in prior experiences that waiting on God is a part of my relationship with Him. It will bring answers and build character when I practice patience. But if I am in a stressful season and the answers from Him don't arrive, I will need to calm myself and learn to trust Him again, but on a deeper level.

Having resilience means that I choose to take responsibility for the part I play in each circumstance. I may see myself as not having or being enough to meet the demands of a crisis. But seeing my lack works to my advantage if I am also able to see the possibilities for growth that a difficult issue can bring with it.

What can I hope to gain from difficult circumstances? My knowledge of God will grow and my awareness of my limitations will grow. Through difficulties I can develop aspects of myself that may otherwise have been left dormant. I can depend on God in new-found ways, change my outlook, and learn wisdom. I can discover that I am able to rise after falling and even walk forward.

If a situation demands more physically, emotionally, or spiritually than I currently have, I can admit that both to myself and to God. Having lack reminds me that my sufficiency is not in myself. It shifts my focus from myself to God. That assessment helps me to see my part of a situation and then do my part. I begin to realize that I am not a victim. I will have a role to play, a decision to make, and some steps to take in assuming responsibility in the crisis at hand.

I had to hold on to God's strength because I had none of my own. I gained resilience and my faith grew from the first round of breast cancer, but I was pressed into the edges of that faith when I was diagnosed with Stage IV cancer ten years later. I held the same resilient faith then, but my faith was being stretched. I had to ask for faith when doubts plagued me. It was in my lack of faith that God met me, supplying what I lacked. I identified with Mark 9:24: "I do believe; help me overcome my unbelief!"

Faith is not built in a vacuum. It grows in the tight constraints of our overwhelming circumstances. When we are confronted with doubts and choose to trust God anyway, faith grows. It is confidence in God's character to be who He has said He is. It is not always having our way. It is not believing that the circumstances will work out to our liking. But it is believing that He knows the way, regardless of the circumstance. When we innocently ask God for more faith, He provides us with a situation that requires more than we have. Some people call it a test. I call it a greenhouse. Your need for

God and your need to mature in your faith is when challenges seem to come.

———————

Faith is not built in a vacuum. It grows in the tight constraints of our overwhelming circumstances.

———————

It is God's faith that lives within us. We certainly didn't create it. He forms it in us when we require it. Our part is to be open to His process of growing faith in us. I know there are folks walking around with a greater measure of faith than I have. They seem to be confident in every situation. Perhaps theirs is truly a gift of faith. But for the rest of us, there is the process God uses to grow faith in us. When there is a situation that requires more faith than we currently have, be confident that God is at work, infusing greater faith in you. The God-breathed inception of faith is given when it is required.

I am traveling with you as I write this book. Together we will follow the principles and strategies that encourage our choosing to say yes to God in simple ways. His track record of transforming those who follow Him through cataclysmic circumstances is historically documented. He walks with us during these hard places, not merely helping us pick up the pieces after they pass. But more. He brings us into a redemptive place to receive wisdom, hope and a greater ability to trust Him. This is the resilience we are after. This is the resilience we need.

No matter the crisis at hand or the one I've just come through, my desire is to move forward with a different perspective and a deeper abiding trust in God. Are you in that same place? No matter what failing or falling you and I have experienced, desiring to get back up and walk with God is the goal. You may be looking for a way to move forward with Him today. In this way we are on the same journey. We want to develop resilience and transform in the process of navigating through struggles. We want to gain from these experiences no matter how difficult they are.

That is exactly what God wants for us. He desires that we are changed through the crisis. If we hold on to Him, He promises redemption in the form of real and eternal transformation. He equips us through the hard places, but He never intends for us to stay in them. He teaches us to move on with Him, to gain wisdom and develop a stronger character through each hardship we experience. My prayer for you, and for myself, is this: "I keep asking that the God of our Lord Jesus Christ, the glorious Father, may give you the Spirit of wisdom and revelation, so that you may know Him better."

We can come through adversity with a deeper knowledge of the God we serve. Our trust in Him grows as we walk with Him through difficulties. Paul continues: "I pray also that the eyes of your heart may be enlightened in order that you may know the hope to which he has called you, the riches of his glorious inheritance in the saints." Paul compares the strength given to us as being like that which "raised Christ from the dead" (Ephesians 1:17-20).

When we hold fast to God through trials and hardship, we experience the strength of God and over time are transformed. Slowly, and almost imperceptibly, this change happens as we live our lives with Him. His nature becomes ours as we continue to weather the storms and choose His ways to navigate through them. God's rescuing us doesn't mean He will prevent all pain and hardship. When we abide with Him in our crisis, in our messiness, in our layers of vulnerability, we acquire Christlikeness. His nature is promised to us *as* we continue to hold onto Him through the struggles.

You may notice that you don't handle things quite the same way. You don't faint from the pressure. You still feel the sensations and the fatigue from it all. But you gather hope as you experience the crisis. Your hope is being built as you are finding your next step. You are bending from the pressure, not breaking. As you take two steps forward and a few back, you are being changed into His image by the Spirit of God. (See 2 Corinthians 3:18.)

If you're coming out of a hurtful relationship, embarrassed by falling into debt, disappointed by work performance, and have more fear than faith when facing these circumstances, then let's talk about changes you can make in moving forward. If your current situation is one of turmoil, crisis, or on-going health issues, we both know this: God can redeem, heal, and transform those who open themselves up to Him. Let us walk through the coming pages and put our disbelief in our abilities on the shelf, while we focus on God's ability to do the impossible through us. Keep your heart and mind open and willing to find the purpose and redemption that God promises.

Willingness to change, adapt, and grow

Think of the most resilient characters in scripture. Did you think of Hannah who persistently prayed for a child and never gave up? Or Job, who held fast to God's goodness when he suffered incredible loss? Or Esther, who risked her life as she pleaded for the lives of her people? Or Joseph, who forgave great injustices from his brothers? Or did you think of Paul who continued to preach the gospel after being stoned and persecuted? They demonstrated persistence, endurance, recovery from hardship, and an intense focus on purpose.

In our day, resilient faith may show up differently from these heroes of faith, but the qualities of resilient faith are the same. When we can make changes and recover from crisis or traumatic experiences, when we use godly wisdom to support our faith while persisting, when we continue to be faithful despite hardship or struggles, we are acting with resilient faith. It is actively operating in us as we bend to meet the challenges without breaking our commitment to God or giving up. It is flexing as we make choices to use wise strategies that support our faith while letting God lead us through a difficult season. Resilient faith grows in that difficult season as we hold onto Him.

Today, how would you rate your own resilience? Are you hanging onto faith by a thread, hoping that your circumstances get better? Are you proving your faith by praying for ways to navigate with God and watching for His response? Or are you checking out through binge scrolling, a rom-com series, or other handy distractions? Do you just want relief from the barrage of stressful struggles?

I want to offer you ways to confront a crisis even as it unfolds. By the end of this book, you will be more aware of your options for moving through difficulties, you will seek ways to apply the strategies that support faithfulness, and you will be grounding the resilient faith you have and strengthening the faith you need for the future.

We build resilience when we make a crucial decision: to get back up after a fall. In deciding not to stay knocked down, even if we must struggle to get up, we've already begun to build resilience in acting on that decision. In the face of adversity, resilience is the willingness to adapt, change and to grow. We are not born with it, but it can be developed and encouraged by our choices.

Spiritual resilience is using faith in God to support our ability to "bounce back."

Spiritual resilience is using faith in God to support our ability to "bounce back." Faith and resilience work together. We grow as we draw on God's strength in navigating through a hardship and in getting back up afterwards. We navigate through difficulties with greater hope in Him and the work He is doing in our lives. We lean into Him for strength. In doing so, we move forward.

Michael Ungar, a family therapist, and resilience researcher at Dalhousie University, agrees that resilience is the ability to not just bounce back after difficulties, but to move forward and grow. In a magazine interview with Wendy Helfenbaum, Ungar said we don't go back to "normal" after a difficult event. "Nobody ever goes back to the same normal; you're changed by your experience," he said, "What we now understand is that you are more or less resilient depending on the circumstances and the resources you have around you."[2]

Our resilience is built on the resources that we use daily. The source of our faith is God. He strengthens us and guides us daily. He uses the pressure of circumstances to transform us. In the struggles God helps us see our need for His strength and guidance. Over time we increase our ability to withstand doubt, remove stressful onslaughts and trust Him. We come to know Him in ways we wouldn't have without the pressure of those circumstances.

If you have vacillated between the fear resulting from severe crisis and the life of calm that you are praying for; if you cannot remember the last time you were not looking for the proverbial next shoe to drop; if you want to sense that everything will be alright, but don't know how to get back to a sense of normalcy, then you are ready for the promise that God gives us all. He will build resilience in you in the middle of the crisis. He will create in you a hope that will not disappoint. He is building tenacious faith in you that can stand strong, even in your weakest moments. That is the promise of resilience. That resilient person is you. As you read the strategies offered, you will see how they can support you spiritually. You will select strategies that work for you, helping you to move forward. You will increase your capacity to face future stress. You will be building resilience that will support your faith.

When her husband of eleven years suddenly died, Sheryl Sandberg was overcome with grief. Even after months of mourning, she and her two children could not function. The crisis left them hopeless and paralyzed. Finally, she sought the help of her friend, psychologist, Adam Grant, and what resulted was their book, *Option B: Facing Adversity, Building Resilience and Finding Joy.* Adam encouraged Sheryl to take concrete steps to recover and bounce back from the life-shattering circumstances. In their book, they shared two clear facts. One, we are not born with a fixed amount of resilience. And two, it is a muscle that everyone can build.[3]

When we face a crisis, we can feel as though the joy of living has been replaced by a frantic scramble to function. Add multiple adverse events that show up at the same time and the darkness seems to deepen. Our faith can feel like a thin rope. But it is in our weakest times of faith, we know God is ready and able to give grace and strength. God is more than enough. He has a plan for building resilience through a crisis. Romans 5:3-5 says: "but we also glory in our sufferings, because we know that suffering produces perseverance; perseverance, character; and character, hope. And hope does not put us to shame, because God's love has been poured out into our hearts through the Holy Spirit, who has been given to us." He forms life-giving resilience in us when we follow Him no matter the circumstances.

God works things together for good

Having resilient faith is not just about getting back up. It's about believing that God's larger plan for us is to use difficulties to form us into the image and likeness of Jesus. It is using our faith to believe that He is working His character into us through the struggles. He uses all things to work together for our good for that transformation to take place. "All things work together for good to them that love God, to them who are called according to his purpose." (Romans 8:28, KJV) Can we believe that our falls, our mistakes, and lack of success are all included in the things He uses to bring His good plan into our lives?

Our broken world brings turmoil, chaos, and difficulties. But God uses these adverse issues to help us grow. They are not good in and of themselves. But in His hands and in our faith-walk with Him, He uses them to transform us into His image and form His nature in us. He uses them to teach us to tenaciously hold on to Him.

Jeremiah 29:11 says, "God has a plan for good and not for evil, to give us a hope and a future." (NLT) In a world where there are economic pressures, disease, and societal problems, is He offering us opportunities even in hardship, to make the light of our lives shine even more brightly? Could His purpose for us be to become more resilient and grow in the face of these conditions? Will He use the crisis you are going through for good and not for evil? He does and He will. God uses the crisis of our lives as part of His good plan.

Michele Cushatt, in her book *I Am*, clarifies what God does and doesn't always do. "You've likely lived long enough to know that rescue doesn't mean God will prevent all pain and hardship. Unexpected life still happens, even when God is in it. No, God doesn't always rescue us from harm, but He always rescues us in it. (Go ahead and read that again.)"[4]

Our perspective about suffering and crisis relates to our core beliefs about God's goodness. If we are certain that He is good no matter what, it will buoy us up in any storm.

There is deep love at the core of all that God does and allows. When our faith is challenged, found lacking, and then built stronger by our leaning into Him, His love is at work. Resilient faith is built in much the same way as muscle is built in a gym. We challenge our muscles with resistance or weight. This breaks down the muscle fibers. As they heal, they grow stronger. In the same way, repeated challenges to our faith provide opportunities to grow by resisting doubt and holding fast to God. We see His love at work as we resist letting go, giving in, or compromising.

We can grow from the circumstances that come our way as we hold onto Him. In John 15:5 Jesus reminds us of our need to stay connected to Him. "I am the vine; you are the branches. If you remain in me and I in you, you will bear much fruit; apart from me you can do nothing." Instead of being offended when these challenges face us, we can look at hardship as God's love meeting us right where we live, in order to transform us. We hold fast to Him as we persist through the difficulties. We bear the fruit of His Spirit in persevering and continuing with Him.

Choosing grace

Suffering can feel inevitable when a crisis hits. My emotions are on high alert. Will I take flight, fight, or freeze? In the anxious moments, when I can feel the pressure is on, my emotions can become my worst enemy. Are you like I am in a crisis? Fighting the temptation to give up? Are you failing and falling in the thick of it? Then do you step into judgement of yourself to take back some sense of control? Do you criticize yourself when you aren't able to control the circumstances? When we don't measure up in faith or life, it's easy to blame ourselves. We start doubting the strength of our faith, hoping to self-correct, thinking we are helping.

All the while, this difficult experience is forming and transforming our hearts. The Bible tells us that our crisis and traumatic experiences hold the possibility of our faith being purified like gold: "But he knows the way that I take; when he has tried me, I shall come out as gold." (Job 23:10, ESV) God's promise motivated Job even in the extreme trauma he experienced. The promise of coming through and being transformed set Job up to not judge himself. His friends came and harshly judged Job. But God gave grace to Job from the beginning. God's plan was for Job to fight for the goodness of God in the form of grace as the way to move through the hardships.

Instead of judging myself, what if I choose that same grace? Not the contemporary kind of grace that excuses us from obedience or our responsibility, but grace to fuel our obedience to God, making a way to stay connected to Him. That grace can be a source of building hope. In the middle of a crisis, as I take on an infusion of God's grace, I am filled with life-sustaining hope right when I need it most. Allowing myself to receive from Him in the middle of suffering means I can choose to let go of my control. I can course-correct. I can choose not to try harder or try to think my way through the issue, even when things seem out of control.

Choosing God's grace while navigating a crisis teaches me resilience. God is making a way for me. As I receive grace, I am receiving His path forward. I have more than myself to rely on. I have His promises to assure me of His truth. I have His power in my weakest moments. When I choose to let go of my control, I open myself to God. His grace gives life and hope because I sense I belong to a power beyond this world. It is not all on me to make it through, to be tougher or stronger. It is God at work through me. As I face the hardships, I receive His grace.

The journey to renew our mind

When I was five years old, I busted my lip falling off my bike and onto my handlebars. Despite the risks, I continued to ride. I would have an occasional accident, but I built skills as I continued. Through the years, I have learned how to ride on trails through rugged terrain, pump my way up tough inclines, and enjoy the feel of the wind blowing through my hair as I glided back down. Falling became part of the learning process. It did not determine how and if I would continue. More recently, I began to wonder if riding was still for me. I fell and didn't get back up with the same ease I used to. My age challenged my perspective about bike riding, but I felt that if I trained and built stronger legs and balance, I could safely continue.

You and I fall through mistakes, sin, and unpredictable situations taking us by surprise. None of those are meant to stop or derail our faith in God. By preparing our hearts and minds through disciplines of scripture and prayer, God will strengthen our capacity to build faith, enabling us to stand in the face of adversity. He will bring us greater resilience.

God offers us a life-long journey with Him. He uses all our experiences to form us into the image and likeness of Jesus. This journey is a long and winding road. Our ability to go the distance starts with what the Bible calls renewal. "Do not conform to the pattern of this world but be transformed by the renewing of your mind." (Romans 12:2) We renew our minds by replacing ingrained lies with the truth of God's Word.

This mind reset is the first step we will look at in forming resilience. In 1 Corinthians 2:16 it says, "But we have the mind of Christ and do hold the thoughts (feelings and purposes) of His heart." (AMP) Forming the mind of Christ is a daily process. It is holy, meaning set apart for His purposes, and it is a lifelong process.

God is with us in this mysterious plan for our transformation. Like a masterpiece painted in small brush strokes, He works on us consistently with great interest. He offers us a new mind, a tender heart, and a self-disciplined nature. We are being conformed into the image and likeness of Jesus. The mindset strategies we will explore in the coming pages will be tools to carry with us for life. In turn, our renewed mind will impact our physical health, our relationships, and our ability to become more resilient.

The promise of resilience

Second Corinthians 3:18 says, "But we all, with open face, beholding as in a glass the glory of the Lord, are changed into the same image from glory to glory, even as by the Spirit of the Lord." (KJV) The Lord builds resilience in one who follows His lead. We move from glory in Him to glory repeatedly. With each crisis or challenge God accomplishes transformation. Even if we fall, we learn. Even if we fail, we grow. Even though we are feeling the pain of loss, we are in the middle of another step forward. We are getting back up and moving forward.

In Oliver Wendell Holmes' poem "Chambered Nautilus," these last lines express our journey in building resilience.

Build thee more stately mansions,

O my soul,

As the swift seasons roll!

Leave thy low-vaulted past!

Let each new temple, nobler than the last,

Shut thee from heaven with a dome more vast,

Till thou at length art free,

Leaving thine outgrown shell by life's unresting sea![5]

God sees each one of us as a stately mansion that goes from glory to glory. We leave our outgrown shells behind because they do not serve us. Do you see the person you are becoming? Can you see yourself through His eyes? You are being built into a new creation, a more resilient one. One that falls and gets back up with greater resilience, that can bend without breaking. You are being transformed as you trust the Lord.

TAKEAWAYS

- The amount of resilience we have is not fixed at birth. We learn to acquire it through the choices we make about the adverse circumstances that we face.
- Struggle is the prerequisite to growing resilience.
- Resilience is the ability to make changes and recover from stressful or traumatic experiences. It is the ability to adapt, change and to grow.
- God's rescuing us doesn't mean God will prevent all pain and hardship.
- God will transform us as we remain connected to Him through life's inevitable hardships.

SPIRITUAL PRACTICE: JOURNALING

Find a quiet place. Journal about one or more of the following questions:

What are some of the ways you strengthen your faith when times are especially difficult?

What are some of the ways you have weakened your faith when you struggled?

What are some ways your hope in God's goodness brings security to you when things seem out of control?

CHAPTER 2
Thinking Outside the Box

Be made new in the attitude of your minds.

–Ephesians 4:23

THE FIRST DAY of school is wild. Even though I'd been teaching middle school art for seven years, I always found the energy of that first day made me question my calling to teach. Everyone's a little off kilter wondering which way to go. Giggles and loud outbursts line the halls. Cheap cologne and sweat swirl in anticipation. Wide-eyed tweeners vie for center stage or a corner where they can hide. The air is buzzing with nervous energy. They flood the art room, competing for back row seats. Trying to talk with my students for the first time is a little like making conversation with a stranger. It begins in earnest but could get awkward quickly.

All the chatter stops as I start my first conversation with them as a class: "How do we think outside the box?" A small girl sitting front and center perks up in a timid voice, "What is 'the box'?" I realize she may be speaking for the entire class. I walk to the whiteboard and draw a very large square. "This is a symbol of who you are. It represents your music, who you choose to be your friends, and your favorite colors. It contains what you think is important and how you think of yourself."

Soon they discovered how their in-the-box thinking could impact their learning. Whether we focused on sculpting, watercolor painting or designing tennis shoes, I taught them to notice the negative comments and thoughts about their abilities and how to choose to override them. If they thought they always painted badly, then that mindset limited their learning new art skills. If they could think differently about themselves and the possibilities of improving their skills, they could focus on the technique of painting, for example, without the extra obstacle of thinking that they were not good at it. It was when they forgot about their self-imposed limited thinking that they enjoyed creating art the most.

Choosing a new mindset

You may be thinking, "if only our thinking could be changed as easily as that!" Who can do something as small as changing their thoughts and expect to see life-changing results? The truth is anyone can. It is as simple as creating a new habit. Small steps can seem like we are moving slowly. Progress can seem arduous and the changes small. But all of us change by taking small, yet continuous steps in a new direction. It is the same with developing a new mindset. It is accomplished one step at a time. Small steps forward ensure growth.

The Bible repeatedly invites us to adopt a growth mindset. We read that admonishment in 2 Peter 3:18: "But grow in the grace and knowledge of our Lord and Savior Jesus Christ."

Growth mindset treats failure as a step toward progress. Perseverance is the characteristic needed if we are to gain maturity. James 1:4 reminds us: "Let perseverance finish its work so that you may be mature and complete..." Growth mindset sees challenges as opportunities for growth, not as setbacks. Scripture also tells us that challenges lead to growth and maturity.

When we notice the fixed or in-the-box ways of thinking, we can take small steps to replace that mindset. Incorporating a growth mindset into our thinking builds resilience and develops a strong faith. It is doable and worth the adjustments. Using it helps us navigate through life's hurdles, problem-solve without self-blaming, and consider the possibilities in moving forward after a crisis. A growth mindset helps us to bravely follow God, even when we feel inadequate or afraid.

Let's look at three people who were challenged by God's plans for their future. How did their preconceived ideas about themselves restrict God's purposes for their lives? Did they have a fixed mindset, or a growth mindset? When God pulled them from their box of self-perceived limitations, they grew in resilience and accomplished much.

The reluctance of Moses, Jeremiah, and Gideon

God called Moses after years of him hiding in the wilderness. God directed him to lead the Israelites out of Egyptian slavery and into the Promised Land. But Moses had been living as a shepherd and was keenly aware of his shortcomings. When he heard what God wanted him to do, he answered from the box he lives in. "Who am I that I should go to Pharaoh and bring the Israelites out of Egypt?" So, God assured him, "My Presence will go with you." in Exodus 33:14-16. Did that nudge Moses out of his box? No. Moses found another reason to resist God's call. "O Lord, I have never been eloquent...I am slow of speech and tongue... Please send someone else to do it." (Exodus 4:10) In response, God sends Aaron to speak on his behalf and Moses reluctantly steps outside of his box to obey.

Jeremiah was also reluctant to say yes to God. When God told him, "I have appointed you as a prophet to the nations." Jeremiah said, "Ah, Sovereign Lord, I do not know how to speak; I am only a child." (Jeremiah 1: 6-8, KJV) The box that he came from limited his desire to obey God.

When an angel delivered God's call to Gideon, he was reluctant as well. God told him to deliver the Israelites from the Midianites, but he had second thoughts: "But Lord, how can I save Israel? My clan is the weakest...and I am the least in my family." (Judges 6:15)

The box that Gideon lived in limited his ability to see what God saw in him.

In each of these situations, God delivers a call, and the receiver is reluctant because of the limitations they put on themselves. Was it that each of them misunderstood God's instruction? Or was it fear that limited their ability to respond to God? Moses, Jeremiah, and Gideon resisted God's call initially, just as I can resist God's leading in even smaller, everyday issues. If it is a new job, meeting a new group of people, or learning a new computer skill, I can resist or even refuse. If I am stressed, I can allow my feelings to color my obedience. If my last job has been challenging, if our family is navigating financial difficulty, or there is an unresolved health crisis, I can resist saying yes to God. The circumstances can overwhelm my ability to see outside the self-limiting box of circumstances.

About a year before my first cancer diagnosis, God offered me an opportunity to learn about how fear and negative self-talk could keep me from obeying Him. He knew the challenges that lay ahead and graciously taught me a big lesson. My husband and I attended a large church at the time. One Wednesday night, at a prayer meeting of about eight people, the Lord gave me some insight into the difficulties our community had been having. I shared it for prayer.

Afterwards the pastor asked me to meet him, and he invited me to share these insights with the whole congregation that Sunday. At first, I was afraid. This was a large church, and lay members had never been asked to share spiritual input from the Lord. As the days passed, the fear only grew. Would I be able to articulate what I needed to say without literally trembling?

In the days leading up to Sunday, the Lord took me through scripture that made me aware of how fear could short-circuit obedience. Specifically, Isaiah 41:10 calmed and shifted my focus. "So do not fear, for I am with you; do not be dismayed for I am your God. I will strengthen you and help you; I will uphold you with my righteous right hand." I was not alone. God was giving me instruction. I needed His compassion and confirmation to obey Him. He did not judge me for being afraid, instead He helped me to look at the fear head-on and obey Him despite my feelings. His strength became my strength. Trusting His lead moved me beyond my self-imposed box of limitations. It helped me to see myself through His eyes, as one who can walk by faith, not allowing fear to prevent me from obeying Him.

You've probably faced many situations where fear has threatened to stop you in your tracks. As God met you then, did He clear your mind, strengthening your commitment to Him? Did He diminish your feelings of inadequacy and help you do what you could not do in your own strength? Did He make you braver than you naturally are? As you set aside your self-imposed limitations, He proves His place in your life, as provider, defender, and lover of your soul.

These Old Testament heroes began with reluctance to God's call, but they didn't stay there. They did not continue to resist God because they wanted to honor Him. God showed them that His purposes were larger than their excuses. His presence would be with them, and they would obey whether they felt inadequate in themselves or not. He was patient and responded to their needs.

In the same way, God has infinite patience with us. He is not put off by our hesitancy. He will meet us right where we are. He had larger plans and purposes for these Old Testament heroes. He has unimaginable plans and purposes for our lives as well. God has a distinctly different perspective of each of us than we may have of ourselves. He has hopes and dreams for us that we may not have considered before.

Having a limited human perspective, we can misunderstand or fear God's direction. But as we seek Him, we can learn to say yes to Him, despite our misunderstandings or our fears. Just as God showed Moses, Jeremiah and Gideon, His presence goes with us. As we remove the limitations, we put on ourselves, we are free to receive God's direction and fear not.

Think, then act

A growth mindset leads us not just to think, but to act. The leaders of our church sensed God directing us to plant a church. People from various sectors of the body, including myself, were getting the same message in prayer, which confirmed this calling.

Of course, we engaged in months of discussion and planning. Was the Session (the elder board) going to build a mission church? Were the lay leaders going to follow the assistant pastor in forming it? Or was the congregation going to support that new church plant? The Session agreed to move forward, then inexplicably changed their position and backed away from the plan.

Even as they let go of the idea, the Lord persisted to direct us toward the new church plant. To seek the Lord, several of us traveled to Montreat, NC to an ecumenical retreat. The speakers included John Wimber, the founder of the Vineyard movement. As God would have it, the associate pastor in our group met with John. They prayed for specific answers about the church plant. Because of the perseverance in leadership to seek God and not give up, Coastal Community Vineyard was birthed and grew to 800 members within months. It would become the foundational beginnings for missionaries to Russia and Ethiopia and for another Vineyard church in western North Carolina.

Changing denominations was certainly "out of the box" thinking for these careful Presbyterians. But it was clear to us that this was the way forward. Taking action on God's calling strengthened us for the challenges that lay ahead as we built a new church within a new denomination.

Instead of relying only on our grit and determination, believers have God as our resource for personal resiliency. The Bible tells us that God is our source. When trials threaten us with discouragement and confusion, we go to the Lord who provides the guidance for the way through the struggles, strength to endure as it persists, and grace to trust Him in the process.

A growth mindset strategy

Why do some people seem to accomplish more than others? What causes some to embrace challenges and rise to meet them, while others give up?

Psychologist Carol Dweck spent decades researching those questions, and her work led her to realize that people have either a growth mindset or a fixed mindset. As you can imagine, a growth mindset allows people to learn new things. But more importantly, a growth mindset can be taught. You can even teach it to yourself! The implications for building resilience are profound.

When Dweck coined the term growth mindset, she intended to use her decades of research to influence every sector of society. Her results proved that we can use our mindset to grow and develop. She challenged educational leaders to change how they viewed a child's potential. She demonstrated how to equip artists, engineers, and athletes with a radical way to view their training and their potential.

A growth mindset is the single marker for those who have achieved success in any area of life. It is the belief that anyone can work hard and learn anything from any age or background. In one of Dweck's studies, disadvantaged Native American children outperformed math students from upper economic districts. They were told they would succeed if they worked hard. Teachers would show students how their perspective about trying hard affected their ability to learn. Additionally, they were praised for their efforts and not just their success. They were encouraged to persevere and keep going when the task became hard. This study proved how focusing on our efforts can spark a love of learning and create possibility-thinking, seeing obstacles as a way to increase strength. It focuses on the steps toward the goal, not merely the medal, the race won or the grade.

The results of this and other similar studies have changed attitudes toward how our view of ourselves impacts our accomplishments. It provides scientific proof that perseverance can be developed. In the end, the disadvantaged group did learn to work hard, and they did outperform the economically advantaged group. Having this type of perseverance and believing that you can improve has impacted education, art, and sports. Believing you can grow by working hard sets you up to achieve. This is the power of a growth mindset. But the focus isn't on working harder to achieve. Instead, it is learning to be open-minded about our potential to learn, grow, and develop. If you believe you can grow and develop, you are resilient.

If I am open to the possibility of learning a subject and am reminded that I can learn if I am willing to learn, then I will fulfill that intention. However, Dweck's twelve years of research proved, if I limit myself to past failures or belief that I don't have what it takes to succeed, I will limit my possibilities.

This limiting belief is what Dweck called a fixed mindset. Believing that our abilities stay the same is what limits achievement. Those that say "I can't do this" operate from inside a box of limitations, which becomes a self-fulfilling prophecy. They might believe that others are talented, gifted or called by God, but don't see themselves that way. These beliefs are self-limiting and self-fulfilling.

On the other hand, the opposite proved to be true by growth mindset researchers. They found that if we believe that unlimited possibilities await us, if we choose to work hard and learn, then in fact, that will also become self-fulfilling. The way we view ourselves impacts how we approach difficulties and if we grow from our struggles or are limited by them.

In her book, *Mindset: The New Psychology of Success*, Dweck writes: "People are all born with a love of learning, but the fixed mindset can undo it."[1]

Change is difficult. Situations change and require our ability to cope and learn new ways to move forward. The way we view ourselves equips us to work with God in faith while we traverse hard and complex problems. God is with us in this journey. But our beliefs about our ability to be faithful and persevere play a big role in how we tackle difficult circumstances. Do we see ourselves as unable to adjust, find solutions, or be flexible in navigating through a traumatic circumstance? We may be asking questions about ourselves, wondering if we are cut out for the changes involved in consistently taking God's Word as truth, believing that we can rebound after loss, or maintain hope when everything around us is falling apart. Believing that God is with us is to believe we are able to know Him in the hardships of life. It means we believe in our ability to walk by faith, stay the course, fall and get back up and grow in faith when difficult things happen.

God believes in you. He believes that you are more than able to do what you haven't done before. He has a purpose for what we experience. The practical ways of building a growth mindset offers us inroads to developing strength for that journey. Gaining resilient faith grows confidence and growth mindset grows adaptability, possibility-thinking, and endurance. One contributes to the other in a cooperative, infinite loop.

Gaining resilient faith grows confidence and growth mindset grows adaptability, possibility-thinking, and endurance. One contributes to the other in a cooperative, infinite loop.

When we believe that we can tackle a situation with God, we are taking the first crucial steps in gaining resilience. I believe everyone is born with the ability to grow in our faith in God. As we grow, we can become stronger and more mature in our relationship with God. Having a resilient faith means believing we can face hardships with hope, maneuver through problems with God's guidance, and meet life challenges. As we persevere in the face of obstacles, resilient faith will keep growing to meet the difficulties. This happens in an on-going way not because of our strength, but because God is our source of strength. His strength does not run out. The Bible promises: "Certainly the Lord watches the whole earth carefully and is ready to strengthen those who are devoted to Him." (2 Chronicles 16:9, NET)

And God's Word also reminds us: "Let endurance have its perfect effect so that you will be perfect and complete, not deficient in anything." (James 1:4, NET)

How can our lives as believers benefit from Dweck's research? We know God is the source of our strength. But what we believe about ourselves can limit our faith. If God believes that I can grow and become more than I think I can, who should I believe? God or my self-limiting mindset? Can I believe that I can grow into what He is calling me to?

I can use faith to free myself from a limited mindset. I can trust God to grow me into the call, if I am not limited by my past failures, weaknesses, or perceived abilities. If I let go of limiting beliefs about myself, I can grow and change by collaborating with God. Growth mindset works hand-in-hand with resilient faith, and indeed builds resilient faith. As I respond in faith to the hardships, crisis, and difficulties I face, God will build resilience in me.

My husband and I were involved as lay leaders in our new church plant. I was leading the leadership team, and mourning the death of my dad, when I found the lump. Even as I began chemo, I continued to serve as a leader. Like Moses, Jeremiah, and Gideon, I was reluctant. But God freed me from a limited mindset. I chose to believe God for a growth mindset. That season was challenging, but God was faithful.

However, growth does not mean having no boundaries. Eventually it became clear to me that I needed to balance service and rest. I was going through chemotherapy, for heaven's sake. God reminded me that it was okay to take a break. Sometimes the step of growth is to listen to God's invitation to say no when it's appropriate. Sometimes obedience looks like choosing to set a boundary.

If you have ever tried to learn a new skill and gave up because it became too hard, you've experienced the effects of a limiting mindset. You can make a choice to quit or to work at it and persevere. If you keep putting effort into the task and push past the difficulty, you will learn. "Put yourself in a growth mindset. Picture your brain forming new connections as you meet the challenge and learn. Keep on going," Dweck writes. Notice that success comes not just from effort, but from changing your beliefs about what that effort will accomplish. Resilience is learning to keep going no matter what we are facing. We learn to bend and flex, to fall and get back up with the strength God provides.

The Bible reassures us that God partners with us in that growth.

"Being confident of this, that He who began a good work in you will carry it on to completion until the day of Christ Jesus." (Philippians 1:6) He is our advocate, guide and provider in every adversity that comes our way. His promise is to continue with us in all of life, no matter how difficult or how impossible a situation can seem. We go over these hurdles, not just to see how high we can jump. Each difficulty is offered as an opportunity to increase, strengthen, and secure resilience. We are becoming more complete as we hold on to Him through every situation. This is part of His plan. Letting go of our limiting perceptions is our part in that plan.

Pathways that create mindsets

Our brains are a network of gathered and stored neural pathways. This network is created by both your body and your thoughts. You think a new thought and a new pathway is created. Each time a thought is repeated, the brain thickens the white myelin coating on that nerve pathway to accent its importance. The more that thought is repeated, the more likely it is to be remembered.

These functions have been taking place in our brains our entire lives. While we were learning to walk, talk and say please and thank you, our brains were forming these pathways. Over time white matter thickens around the pathways that are travelled the most by our repeated thoughts. Every neuron in our brain goes through the same pathway construction.

The brain does not give a moral or ethical rating system to our thoughts. Repetitive negative thoughts are given the same myelin coating as positive thoughts. If you want to replace negative thoughts, ones that seem to come from nowhere and wake you up at 3 a.m., what do you do? You give it competition. You begin storing positive thoughts and creating new neural pathways. When you intentionally think different thoughts, you can literally change your brain physiology. Eventually, the negative pathway is used less, and the new positive pathways will line with myelin, giving you a more positive mindset. These positive thoughts are not just positive affirmations we tell ourselves. They include any thoughts that are not self-limiting or condemning.

What better way to eliminate negative thinking than to use scripture to create new pathways! By repeating scriptural truths to compete with these negative pathways, we offer our brains hopeful and life-supporting nutrition. This is the foundation of how our beliefs are formed. As we input God's truth into our brains, we begin to sense the difference that scripture is making in our thinking. Soon our negative thoughts are outnumbered by the positive ones created by scripture. We use the ancient paths that saints have used for eons, reading and meditating on scripture. It's amazing how meditating on scripture makes more sense just by learning how the brain works. Its benefits have been there all along. Now we understand how our brains operate to bring about these results.

Using scripture to create a new mindset

Scripture increases our understanding about who God is. We can use scriptural truths to create a positive mindset that will support our walk with God and build resiliency. Carving out time to study scripture will create positive brain pathways and build a resilient faith. You could start by asking God to bring insight and understanding before reading the selected verses. To dig deeper, try opening commentaries to look at a broader context of these verses. Several apps are available with easy access to theologians' writings. Researching the Hebrew or Greek origins of a central word in a verse can also offer a rich understanding of scripture. Themed studies can be used to focus on one word. In using an English thesaurus to find various meanings for the word "hope," for instance, you can see how similar words broaden the understanding of it. You could follow that by searching the reference section of the Bible and look up verses that use the word "hope" in them. The next step could be to take one of these verses that speak to you personally and ask the Lord how to apply it.

For example, I remember meditating on the promise found in Isaiah 26:3-4, "He will keep in perfect peace whose mind is stayed on

Me because he trusts in Me." (ESV) The word "stayed" stuck with me. As I looked up synonyms for it, I came across the word "strut." It is a stabilizing mechanism used both in construction and in a car. A car strut acts as a shock absorber to support the weight of the vehicle and ensure a smooth ride.

In the construction of a roof, the struts are the weight-bearing pieces that are put into place as the roof's pitch is being built. It secures the structure, holding it together. If you think of the pitch of a roof, the strut is found under that point. It ensures that weight is secured while the rest of the structure is being built. I could apply the meaning of the strut to the passage in Isaiah 26. He is promising me His peace as I keep and secure Him, like a strut, in my thoughts, releasing burdens or worries as I go through the day.

Come to think of it, that word strut also illustrates how scripture is used to form our faith. The Word of God works to secure us as we learn, grow, and build a relationship with Him. As we meditate and focus on a verse, it becomes a pathway for our faith to grow. We move beyond where we have been and challenge ourselves to take on what God has provided in the verses. They hold our focus and connect us with the Lord.

Matt Tommey, author and artist, explains renewing our minds this way: Your mind is renewed as you interpret your life "through the lens of God's Word and the inspiration of the Holy Spirit, rather than through the lens of your experience, woundedness, trauma, prefer-ences, or the opinions of others. It's a fundamental shift toward seeing the world, yourself, others, God, and especially what's possible from a Kingdom perspective."[2]

Scripture changes our focus and our perspective by giving us God's viewpoint. It spiritually feeds our hearts and minds as we are being transformed by it. Philippians 2:13 (TPT) describes it best: "God will continually revitalize you, implanting within you the passion to do what pleases Him." This is the grand work of the Holy Spirit growing faith in us through His Word.

Scripture provides insight about how God will use His Word to build our faith. Proverbs 3:6 points out God's faithful guidance to make our paths straight, as we submit our lives to Him. The verses that cause you to stop and think are the very verses to meditate on, study further and memorize. Print them on three by five cards or keep them as a note on your phone. Keep them in your purse, wallet or near your most comfortable chair. Rest in them and take them to heart.

If you have spent time meditating on scripture, you know its power and endless source of strength. It is what God will use to direct, encourage and teach you. From settling our anxiety to seeking specific direction, the Bible offers insight and guidance as you meditate on its meaning. When you seek God's support through scripture, the Holy Spirit guides your steps forward.

John Eldredge underscores the importance of this process in his "Wild at Heart" blog. "Mental resilience begins when we decide to take hold of our thought life. [It is] built by intentionally, consciously saying positive things–which for the believer would be all the beautiful truths of Scripture. Reading and memorizing scripture builds mental resilience because it is a living breathing text in which you encounter God, and through which you get perspective on the world."[3]

Our adventure into God's living and active Word revives our hearts and ignites a perspective that truly is not of this world. We know God's love through scripture. We are given guidance in His Word. Jesus reminds us of our need to receive it in Matthew 7:24, "Therefore everyone who hears these words of mine, and puts them into practice is like a wise man who built his house on the rock." We build our lives on its impenetrable and eternal truth.

An excellent adventure

I was on my own at twenty-three and on the other side of the country when God showed me the box of limited thinking I had been living in. I had a new job and new friends. The small hometown and family I knew were miles away. I was wide-eyed, inexperienced, and looking for a new life. It all seemed like an adventure. At that point I had been a church girl for years. I knew the books of the Bible. I memorized key verses. I knew what blanks needed to be filled in doing church life. But one afternoon in my little apartment on Genevieve Street everything changed. The box that I had put God in disappeared. My structured, inside-of-the-church-building way of thinking about Him no longer existed. My reality shifted.

That afternoon, I was getting ready to head out for a racquetball match. As I sat on the edge of my bed, tying my tennis shoes, I started to feel like I wasn't alone. Then in what seemed like a series of swift scenes from a movie, I began seeing pictures in my mind's eye. I heard a voice say that these scenes represented the times in my life He had protected me. I knew immediately that it was God. Maybe it was because His voice was powerful and gentle all at the same time. He brought to mind a time I'd been driving on a dirt road in southern Louisiana with friends. We drove up on an oil rig that was manned with workers. I didn't know that we were in danger. But God was showing me that He had protected me from harm. The scenes from my past continued. One by one, an image would appear in my mind's eye and God would repeat that He had lovingly protected me.

Suddenly I began to realize the otherness of God. He did not think like I did. I had had no thought of God watching over me during those times. But He had thoughts of me. He was there, providing for me when He was the last thing on my mind.

Did I mention that this was the first time I heard God? I was talking to Him in my thoughts, and He was answering me. Yet, it was the most natural conversation. I simply talked to Him as though I was talking with a friend. That moment with Him changed my life. Because His presence seemed so tangible, I felt He knew me. John 10:27 says "My sheep hear my voice; I know them, and they follow me." God was calling me to follow Him that day. He was proving that He lived outside of my box of set thoughts about myself and about Him.

As the images stopped, God said, "Everything you have, I have given you. But you do not have one thing." *What don't I have?* "You don't have Me!" I sat on the edge of my bed stunned. I knew the Bible that told me about Him. But I had to agree, I didn't know Him at all.

So, I asked God if He would help me know who He was. *Would You take me through the Bible and show me who You are?*

Every morning before work, I would dig into the Word, find a verse for that day and ask Him to show me what it meant. I was not asking Him to provide information. I desperately wanted to know how that verse connected to me in my life then. Every day I would find a different verse and ask the same question. Every day He answered me. Every day He would show me how this verse was personal. These verses were simple. But God would make it clear that He meant them for me. The truth He was conveying was my truth. He showed me it was relevant for my life in real time.

For example, one morning I read in Luke 12:24: "Consider the ravens: They do not sow or reap; they have no storeroom or barn; yet God feeds them. And how much more valuable you are than birds!" God was feeding my spirit as He provided me with a job and the food I ate every day. I thanked Him. Every day I would locate a different verse and ask Him to show me how it meant something to me personally. Every day I knew He was speaking the truth of that verse to me. It was as though He was sending me personalized messages. He saw me, He knew me, and He cared about me knowing it. It was the beginning of an adventure that I could not have imagined. I came out of my box of what I thought I knew and began saying yes to Him.

As we exercise faith in His abilities, we can overcome our in-the-box thinking about our own abilities.

Slowly, day after day with verse after verse, I began to see God's nature through what He was pointing out to me in scripture. This simple practice allowed me to experience God and realize that He was exactly who He said He was. I realized how personal, caring, and gentle He is; how completely supernatural He is. I saw something I had never seen before. God was talking directly to me. He captured my heart by speaking to me through His Word. My life was being moved forward, away from my limited, constricted thinking. I realized that the limitations I put on my learning, growing, and changing are not the ones God puts on me.

Our box of limitations rarely allows us to grow, attempt new things, or think in renewed ways. Our boxes will only offer options from what we have experienced before. They may offer comfort, but that coziness is stifling. By trusting God past our limitations, we begin building a mindset that can hold resilience. As we exercise faith in His abilities, we can overcome our in-the-box thinking about our own abilities.

Growing resilience starts as I say yes to Him. It starts as I allow Him to show me new life found in His Word. He calls me outside the box of my thinking and into new adventures as I walk with Him. He is providing that same infinite adventure for you too.

Growth mindset and beliefs

Small changes in your thinking are as impactful as making course corrections in a ship. Just as the captain of a ship can alter its course by turning the wheel just one degree, we can change our destination with subtle changes. To change the way our brain works, we must feed it differently day by day. Growth mindset is proven science. It helps us see that there may be unlimited possibilities for our future. It challenges our fixed beliefs and creates new ways to grow and transform.

The first step is to examine our thoughts, to become aware of what we actually are thinking about. This is the foundational work of inner transformation. If we pay attention to how we think, we will see where the changes need to be made. In Proverbs 23:7 it says, "as a man thinks... so is he." (AMP) This verse establishes a relationship between what God says about self-thoughts and what Dweck proved in her decades of research. We are what we think, and we do control what we feed our brains. We can choose to speak positively instead of negatively in our internal dialogue. God is ready to help us make these choices and to follow through. But we are the ones that take the initiative and choose to course-correct.

Spiritual director and author Ruth Haley Barton, in her book, *Sacred Rhythms,* writes: "...the Scriptures will penetrate to our very depths, showing us those things about ourselves that we are incapable of knowing on our own due to our well-developed defense structures."[4]

God has ways to overcome even our resistance to growth. His love overcomes denial, distractions, and passivity. He softens us with His love but also shows us ourselves and our need to change. We learn to trust Him, let go of our defenses and receive from Him.

The truth is, we are responsible for how we learn and grow. We are the gatekeepers of our minds. We are actively involved in the transformation process. Proverbs 4:23 tells us to be vigilant to watch what we take in and receive in our hearts which includes our mind, will, and emotions. "Guard your heart with all vigilance, for from it are the sources of life." The renewal of our hearts starts in our minds. Our thoughts create our values. They form our mindsets and our beliefs. Our repeated thoughts inform beliefs. When we change our thoughts, we become aware of what keeps us stuck and what limits our receiving from the Lord. As we change our thinking, we begin to foster growth on the deepest level. The Apostle Paul exhorted believers, "...whatever is true, whatever is noble, whatever is right, whatever is pure, whatever is lovely, whatever is admirable—if anything is excellent or praiseworthy—think about such things." (Philippians 4:8) Focus your mind on what is good, and you notice the positive impact. As you change your mind in this way, you will have a greater desire and ability to obey the Lord.

Fixed mindset in the believer

A growth mindset enables you to grow, change, and develop in all aspects of living. You can fulfill God's call on your life. You must believe that your talent and abilities are not fixed but can be developed throughout your life. If I am a less than enthusiastic learner, I can change that. If I find it hard to memorize scripture, I can change that. "We are more than conquerors through Him who loved us." (Romans 8:37)

The key to scripture memory is to put it in front of you in small bits that speak to you right where you are living today. Then apply what it says and see the truth of what it is pointing out. If you are in need of encouragement, discover a Psalm that brings life and hope. For example, in Psalm 39:7 the psalmist declares that his hope is in God. If you are waiting for an answer from Him and need encouragement, stating your spiritual position before Him could be encouraging. It says: "But now, Lord, what do I look for? My hope is in you." Take those two statements as the focus to stir hope in you. Make it your touch stone when you begin your quiet time. Chew on it and then locate other verses to build on the theme of hope. By meeting a need with the Word in this way, your memorization is serving a dual purpose. It is effecting change as you believe it and it is creating new pathways in your mind.

Faith may begin small, in the size of a mustard seed. But Jesus says that it can move mountains. (Matthew 17:20-21) Sometimes those mountains are the negative ways we think of ourselves. Our thoughts and beliefs about change and growth determine our ability to grow and develop. Taking strategic steps forward in how we think about ourselves offers God rich soil to plant His Word in us.

If we tell ourselves we will never change, then we are fixing ourselves in a cemented mentality. We are putting limitations on ourselves that God never intended. These are the beliefs that keep us stuck and unable to move forward. If we view our limitations as permanent and without a way to overcome them, we are living with a fixed mindset. Ask yourself: are your beliefs about yourself keeping you from believing what God says about you in scripture? If so, you can allow Him to change the way you think about yourself.

Start with self-awareness of the negative self-talk that pollutes your mind and creates resistance to growth. Have you heard yourself saying things like, "I will never be able to do that," or "it's just too hard," or "I am not good at this." Most of us have. When we think these thoughts repeatedly, we are forming a mindset of "I can't" instead of considering what is possible. It is *possible* for you to learn. It is *possible* for you to do hard things. It is *possible* to not be proficient at some task yet and then become better at it given time and effort. Pay attention to what you are saying about yourself in your daily self-talk.

Test your mindset by comparing what you believe about yourself to what God says about you in His Word. Admit the need for change. He will meet you there. Replace your limiting beliefs with His truth. The same way we take steps to change our negative internal dialogue, we can open ourselves to God and not allow limiting beliefs to influence us. Change can start when you ask God to make you aware of the limitations you put on yourself. Repent of doing life your own way and believe that He is right beside you, listening and providing forgiveness and the next steps to a new mindset.

Believe His love for you. Read over the love letters God has written for you. Receive them as personal promises! Wash your brain with those truths!

Next, take steps to reverse the trend. Become aware of your own self-talk. Every time you make belittling or shaming comments about yourself, spin the statement. In your own words, make a statement that allows for change, learning and growth. Let phrases like "it is possible" and "I am not there yet" interrupt the negative statements.

Other ways to incorporate growth mindset into our lives include learning a new skill, embracing those daily problems as opportunities, and challenging yourself to notice your progress in any area of growth instead of only seeing the outcome as the only achievement. Cheer yourself along the way, celebrate your progress, and it will pay off in other areas of life.

Eliminating a fixed mindset assists your ability to trust God. Gradually, you will begin to see difficulties and crises from a different perspective. With God's strength you can meet the challenges that life brings. As it says in Psalm 119:105, "Your word is a lamp to my feet and a light for my path." He leads us in the way we need to go and how we can best live. Our choice is to seek that light through His Word and use it as our guiding light.

We will look at how we can build resilience in facing adversity in the next chapters. You will find ways to create a plan for moving forward no matter the circumstance. You are not alone in facing the pressures of the world we live in. God has infinite ways to offer you help. We will look at some of those as we continue. Through the collected stories and strategies that have proved successful, you will become aware of how resilience is built.

God only thinks of you positively. Psalm 28:7 says, "The Lord is my strength and my shield, my heart trusts in Him and He helps me." Even as He trains and retrains us, He is thinking of our best and of becoming closer to us in that process. Knowing that He views us this way, we can view ourselves as valuable and full of possibility as well. You can trust Him. He is making a way for His strength to meet you wherever you find yourself.

Opening ourselves to the possibilities of change is transformational. It takes the blinders off our hopes and dreams. It removes the limitations we may have about how God could use us. He welcomes each of us with open arms, fully accepting us. By changing negative thinking about our past, our failures, or negativity about current circumstances, we can more easily receive the truth of how God sees us. The offer is always there: you can change your future by removing self-limiting beliefs.

TAKEAWAYS

- Scripture increases my understanding about who God is. I can use scriptural truths to create a positive mindset that will support my walk with God and build resiliency.
- I can change my thinking by offering scripture and positive, life-giving thoughts to myself. This will grow new brain pathways to support resiliency.
- God has a distinctly different perspective of me than I have of myself. He has hopes and dreams for me that I may not have considered before.
- The limitations I put on my learning, growing, and changing are not the ones God puts on me.
- Growth mindset is proven science. It helps me see that there may be unlimited possibilities for my future. It challenges my fixed beliefs and creates new ways to grow and transform.

SPIRITUAL PRACTICE: MEDITATE ON SCRIPTURE

Look at where God takes you over the coming week in scripture. List the key verses or phrases that you read. How do these verses challenge your current thinking about your problems? Use these verses as you pray for guidance, strength, and hope for your week.

Spend some time reading slowly through the stories of Moses, Gideon and Jeremiah in the Bible. What happened when they let go of their fixed mindset? How does their story apply to a challenge you're currently facing?

CHAPTER 3

Willing To Wait

To trust God is to trust His timing. To trust God is to trust His way.

–Lysa Terkeurst[1]

I SAT in my gynecologist's office, trying to keep my dignity while wrapped in a flimsy paper gown. It was June 2001, ten years after my initial breast cancer diagnosis.

"I can't sleep," I told him. "I'm hot, then cold. I have heart palpitations. Something is not right."

He nodded sympathetically but seemed unconcerned. "These are normal symptoms for perimenopause," he said. "You're 49. Most women your age are starting to experience it."

At my insistence, he ran blood tests. All normal. Yet I knew something was off. Then months later, as a final effort to prove to me that nothing was wrong, my gynecologist set me up for a thyroid biopsy. The findings: papillary thyroid cancer.

The thyroidectomy removed the thyroid gland with four thyroid tumors growing on the outside of it. The gland was functioning normally even with the tumors. Next step, the treatment for this cancer, nuclear iodine treatment.

During the treatment for my breast cancer, I had experienced anaphylactic shock in response to contrast dye during a CT scan. Consequently, I knew that there could be issues using iodine. I reviewed these details with my endocrinologist, the hospital nuclear radiologist, and the admitting nurse. Each one assured me I would be given a steroid to combat any allergic responses.

In October, I was admitted to the nuclear treatment facility at New Hanover hospital. Within an hour of swallowing the nuclear iodine capsule, I knew something was not right. My head throbbed. I contacted the on-call doctor at 9:10 p.m. about my pain. At 9:30 my bestie, after clocking out of her nurse-shift at the hospital, checked in on me. No visitors were allowed in the nuclear treatment facility, so we yelled back and forth through the door.

"Finally, the doctor sent Tylenol after an hour of requests. I still have a splitting pain through one side of my head. I'm feeling very strange. Itchy all over and like an elephant is on my chest!"

"You need to keep hitting your call button to remind them. I'll go home and pray!"

"My jaws are tightening, and my throat is… I have to go…"

I ran for the trash can and threw up the liquids I had consumed. I pushed the call button again. But the nurses said it would take a moment to get into their protective haz-mat gear.

Next, I remember lying on the cold linoleum floor. My muscles spasmed causing muscular contractions in waves. My legs and arms flailed, striking out at convoluted angles. My lips swelled and protruded. I gasped for air and screamed for the nurses that now circled around me to help. They stood there in white hooded jumpsuits and watched from about two feet away. After all, I was nuclear.

"Try to stay calm," one nurse encouraged.

After six hours, I was calm. I was exhausted but also aware of what had just happened. I had just lived through my second anaphylactic shock episode. This event clearly proved I would never be able to receive the treatment to eliminate thyroid cancer from my body.

I was out of the hospital on my first trip to get groceries when I ran into a friend and neighbor, Lori.

"What were you doing last Thursday night at about midnight?" she asked.

I thought for a minute. The flashbacks came quickly. "Well, I was in the middle of anaphylactic shock at New Hanover, why?"

Lori turned completely pale and locked eyes with mine. "The Lord woke me up to pray for you. I prayed that you wouldn't die from midnight until about 3.00 am. Now I know why!" She reached out for me. We held onto that hug a little bit longer than usual.

When it continues

I knew God would make a way, but my heart was still plagued with questions: Will I survive? Will I thrive? When will You show me how to walk through these medical issues?

Even when answers didn't appear, I held on to God. The verse "where can I go from your presence?" reminded me that He alone held the answers and that He is my source of healing. If I couldn't have the treatment for thyroid cancer, then He would show me how to live with that truth. I had confronted unresolved issues before: I'd wrestled with depression since my teen years. I knew from that ongoing struggle that God doesn't leave because the battle continues. Just the opposite, I knew He would stay and make good on every other promise He had made me. This was just a different issue. God was the same. He would make a way though I wasn't sure how He would do that.

My battle with depression began when I was in high school. At first, I thought that it was just a bad mood. So did my parents. I was a growing teenager. I just needed extra rest. Even though I was a cheer-leader and active in school sports, served in school government and had plenty of friends, there were days that I stayed in my room, submerged in a book. Then those "bad moods" lasted through college, through first jobs, and through raising children.

Medication caused additional problems. I would go emotionally numb, sleep too much, and couldn't think my way out of a paper bag. I would give up on one medication and start on another one. I would wait the required three to six weeks, check the symptoms and then throw those out too. For seasons when depression overwhelmed me, medicine became an ally. But after years of riding through the ups and downs of trial and error, I gave up and stopped taking them altogether.

My husband struggled to understand my episodes of depression as well. Over the years, we developed a sort of "code" to unpack the day's happenings. When he would walk in the door at night with that exhausted look on his face, I would ask him, "Did you eat the bear or did the bear eat you?"

His tight, drawn face said it all. "I can't talk about it right now" was his hello. What he didn't know is that I had had the same kind of day. That same bear had eaten me. The difference was I needed to talk about it.

To save his need to explain, we had worked out a rating system. Rating it with a number one meant that it was minor. Typical irritations, cranky people, dangerous drivers, repairs that won't stay fixed were his complaints. Enough of those one after another and it may have felt like death by a thousand paper cuts. A day he rated a ten was called "the bear." In his way of looking at it, if he had to talk about the details of his day, he would have to experience it all over again. We had hugely different ways of processing. His way was to leave it at the office.

But I needed to talk about the depression that plagued my day. It had been rough too. Even though we had been through this discussion before, talking about a depressive episode would let me know he was with me. Through our decades of marriage, we're still on two different ends of the processing spectrum. He is on the internal processing end. He worked it out inside his head, and he was fine. I was on the external processing side. Talking about the issue helped me to understand it.

I understand depression is caused by imbalanced chemicals in the brain, but it doesn't make sense spiritually. I have been treated and healed of cancer. But why do I live with depression after years of praying for release from it? I have never seen a cause and effect with the symptoms except when I'm not sleeping well or eating right. Then an episode is almost guaranteed. So, I stick to eight hours of sleep. I eat nutritiously and don't overindulge. I exercise and stick with a walking routine. I can go weeks without a single episode. Then, just when I think I'm over it, it reappears with vengeance.

Though I have talked through the difficulties of managing depression many times, it's still hard for my husband to put himself in my shoes. I get it. It's hard for me to understand it too. When I would talk with my worn-out husband at the end of a "bear" of a day, I kept coming back to wanting him to understand how I felt. I was trying, but I was struggling. I wanted him to see that. I wanted him to see me as heroic for persevering. But am I trying to convince myself that persevering makes a difference? What if it continues this way for the rest of my life? Am I faithful to God in this struggle when nothing changes? I want to be faithful regardless of the struggle. But I want the struggle to have purpose. How about you?

If an ailment, situation, heartbreak, or crisis continues after ongoing prayer, wise counsel, or continuous effort, does it mean that our faith is not enough? When we're waiting for God to bring change do we keep praying or just let go and accept it? What do we do while we wait on God? What do we learn from waiting on Him? Are we giving up if we can't understand His silence? Does the struggle to wait patiently mean we have lost faith? Is bitterness going to result from frustration? How do we become willing to wait on Him? These are the questions we will think through in this chapter. I'll offer faith-filled insight and secure landing places.

Supporting faith in the frustration

Sharing about depression can be empowering. There are myths and misconceptions about depression that bog down faith and require people to live with shame. Our stories hold the potential to free others of that shame and provide hope as they live with this condition. It is an illness. In sharing about this illness, I have seen how it helped people share their journeys of faith. It united our faith to have hope in God as we deal with difficult symptoms. People need to hear what people of faith do in the face of persistent hardship. They want to know how to continue with God when there is ongoing trauma. This is why I'm writing about it now. Your story of continuing with that thing that doesn't get healed or that prayer that doesn't get answered may be different from mine. But it's the perseverance grown from these issues that provides the body of Christ with hope.

Here's the truth. It only takes my faith in God's strength, love, and grace to honor Him. So I ask myself in the middle of the hardest day: "How can I honor God right here, right now? How can I show Him I am believing Him when it looks dark and gloomy from where I'm sitting?" Sometimes it is a worship song, a secular song that I turn into worship (yep, you read that right!), or a statement of gratitude for the privilege of breathing, seeing, or just being alive. Waiting is hard because it feels like doing nothing. But in reality, it is a universal task. Everyone has to wait for something at some time for longer than they may want. But as believers our waiting is a bit different.

My heart attitude is what I give God as I wait. The purpose of this simple act of honoring Him no matter my feelings does not keep me from feeling what I am feeling. But it does help me to fulfill the purpose we all are called to: to glorify God. It begins a shift away from being stuck inside my depression. It gives me a way to get outside of myself. Believe me, God sees and knows my heart during such times. He knows that I am choosing to have faith despite the circumstance. It is one way to exercise some control over the situation.

Further, when I choose to step beyond my condition, I am operating in what a growth mindset calls "not yet." The "not yet" posture is when I am not seeing change but realizing it has not happened *yet*. I don't deny the depressive episode, but I do acknowledge that a turnaround in my symptoms hasn't happened *yet*. That shift in perspective is a notch in the win column. We gain from these successes even though they may seem small. It shifts me from a victim mentality to taking responsibility for my situation. That shift enables me to set priorities and take steps forward throughout the day. These choices help me to glorify God in my condition and make changes in the condition. I may not have changed my circumstances, but I have changed my perspective.

Waiting on God

When I hear the story of how others manage an on-going condition, I believe that I can too. In that same way, I share these details because I want to support you as you navigate through your situation. If the Lord hadn't provided me with the faith to navigate through depression, I wouldn't be able to share this story with hope. However, the resilience built from that condition did not happen quickly. It happened as I allowed myself to receive grace for my circumstances, acceptance of the condition, and have patience while I experienced it. I held onto Him in the misery of what didn't change. But more importantly, He held onto me while I couldn't hold on at all.

When I am in the depths of depression, the Lord meets me right where I am. I am vulnerable and dependent on Him to make it through. It's during these desperate times that I've come to appreciate my deep need for Him. I know where my greatest source of strength lies. I suppose anyone who has learned to come to Him in their weakness, no matter what it is, has learned the strength of that intimate place. He meets us in our weakness. Doesn't He? He comforts us and ministers to us in the depths of our soul.

By waiting *with Him*, and not *on Him* to answer us, we can wait for the timing of His answers.

In God's Word, He promises to meet us: "One thing I ask of the Lord, this only do I seek: that I may dwell in the house of the Lord all the days of my life, to gaze upon the beauty of the Lord and to seek him in his temple. For in the day of trouble he will keep me safe in his dwelling; he will hide me in the shelter of his tabernacle and set me high upon a rock." (Psalm 27:4-5) This is our relationship with Jesus. We are hidden in Him. It is not easy to define. This place of intimacy is the chosen place of our waiting on Him as well. By waiting *with Him*, and not *on Him* to answer us, we can wait for the timing of His answers. We can wait for His healing, patience, and redemption because in that intimate place of waiting, we receive the strength to wait. Because of His love, we can be assured He is always acting from His goodness. No matter how long the waiting continues.

This is how resilient faith is built--by waiting on the promise of God's strength in our times of greatest need. God uses seasons of waiting with Him as a vehicle to build trust, hope, and faith. Our faith is renewed even when it seems the least likely place to build strength. God's goodness sustains us and resilient faith mounts up with eagle's wings just then.

Our world is fixated on speed. Instant gratification. Instant decisions. In business, it's quick turnaround times. On social media, it's short pithy sayings. Ten nanoseconds of bumper sticker truth and we move on to the next meme. Not so with God. He lives beyond time. Instead of running to keep up with us, He arranges the times and the seasons. He sees beyond our immediate needs. His times and directives are based on His purposes. He operates and moves according to a timetable ordered by His goodness and mercy. Theologian and scholar N. T. Wright explains, "God is doing what God is doing in God's time. And, maybe, if we had to slow down a bit we might paradoxically catch up with God."[2] Can we slow down to catch up to God? I believe He meets us as we do.

The goal of waiting on God is to change our attitude, shift our perspective, and relinquish our impatient selves to Him. In her book, *Waiting*, Sharla Fritz writes that we must let go of our will and our timing. "Waiting well means enthusiastically anticipating what God is going to do—even if He chooses a different plan from our own."[3] But how do we change from impatient to expectant as we wait? How do we acquire hope when the waiting itself seems to breed hopelessness?

We need God's encouragement when we are desperate for answers. When we cry out for divine intervention in a difficult relationship, when the healing is delayed, or when starting over after failure doesn't happen, we need the Lord to infuse us with His hope. So, we start from a place of need. We need His help to wait on Him. We need to know what steps to take to build patience and hold on. We even need to know how to pray. He does hear us and in His great love, He comforts us. But as time passes those hopes can grow dim. Impatience can turn to doubt. We may be holding on in faith, but when our struggles remain the same, we can have deeper questions. We ask, "What now, God?"

When we have a question that has a time stamp on it, waiting can feel like it goes on forever. What started as determined, focused, heart-felt prayer has moved and shifted. We are tired. Days can become months. The months become years. Sometimes years have passed and praying with the persistence we once had dwindles. When we are waiting on an answer that God doesn't speak to, waiting itself becomes the issue. Now we fidget when we pray. Just be patient, we tell ourselves. God is in control.

Your will be done

Finding peace and patience in waiting on God requires us to let go. If we choose His will above our own, a dramatic change occurs in our perspective. When we release the thing that needs an answer, placing it in His hands, we notice that our burden and anxiety lessen. Letting go changes our viewpoint. In time the freedom of release becomes real. The attention shifts toward Him. We take our eyes off the problem. We wait on God's will to be done. We exchange what we desire *from* Him to have peace *with* Him. When this shift happens, we receive the very strength we need to wait on Him. We are dependent on the One who has our life in His hands. Because we are focusing on God, we are able to receive restoration for our weary souls. Getting an answer is not the focus, He is.

Sounds simple, right? Simple yes. But in the processing of my heart before Him, I see the issues that keep me from that amazingly simple step. I am faced with a decision: will I allow His will to reign over mine? The key to letting go is relinquishing the answer I seek to Him, to trust Him above my own comfort or control. It is simple, but not easy.

I learned about the act of letting go in a prayer from author Catherine Marshall. She called it the prayer of relinquishment. In her book, *Adventures in Prayer*, she wrote about a time when she had been in bed with a severe lung infection and had prayed fervently for God to heal her. She prayed with everything in her. But even after months there was no change. In fact, her condition got worse. Catherine was at the edge of her faith. Were her demanding prayers separating God's healing from her? She asked and waited for Him to answer.

One afternoon she came across a story of a missionary who was in a similar situation. This missionary was asking God to heal her so that she could serve Him. After eight years in the same condition, she was worn out. She let go of her situation and told Him, "O.K. God! If you want me to be an invalid, that's your business. I want You even more than I want my health."

The missionary's relinquishment of her outcome did not make sense to Catherine who leaned hard into faith as the way to receive healing. But she knew in her heart this was the answer she had been waiting on. "I'm tired of asking," was the beginning of her prayer. "I'm beaten, finished. God, You decide what You want for me."

And the result? "Within a few hours I (Catherine) had experienced the presence of the Living Christ in a way that wiped away all doubt and revolutionized my life. From that moment my recovery began. Through this incident and others that followed, God was trying to teach me something important about prayer. Gradually, I saw that a demanding spirit, with self-will as its rudder, blocks prayer. I understood that the reason for this is that God absolutely refuses to violate our free will; that therefore, unless self-will is voluntarily given up, even God cannot move to answer prayer."[4]

The prayer of relinquishment begins as we surrender our will to the will of our Father. It is an act of letting go of our desires so that His will can happen in our lives. We face the fear of what might happen if our needs are not met. We bend our knees with gratitude that His ways will work for our good, even though we do not know what His ways will be. We place ourselves into the powerful hands of a loving God.

You may have experienced the power of surrender in a similar way.

It's hard to give up wanting what is good and right in our minds. We can want to let go, agree to let go, and then in our very humanness back away from the altar that offers us a place to lay it down. Sound familiar?

Though Marshall's story is different from mine, we both had a need to let go of our requests and hold on to God in the process. We are in relationship with a powerful God who will move toward us in the driest times of our waiting seasons. When we are needy, He will give us faith to hold on. He will comfort us and pick us up when we're down. Because of our waiting, we may see aspects of His character and nature that we did not know before. If we rest in Him as we wait on Him, waiting will have its full effect. We will change.

We bend our knees with gratitude that His ways will work for our good, even though we do not know what His ways will be.

After three years of a complex autoimmune disease, Strahan Coleman, a musician, poet, and spiritual director from New Zealand, came to God out of extreme frustration. The years he spent trying to find treatments brought no relief. His fervent prayers resulted in more questions. Why God, why are there no answers? In his book, *Beholding*, he reflects on the day a dramatic change came. "Something lifted, something I'd been carrying for a long, long time. I don't even know what it was precisely, but it felt like the equivalent of a sports stadium floated off my chest with the ease of a down pillow. Maybe it was my dependence on understanding as a prerequisite to truly experiencing God. Wherever the lift came from, it was the beginning of learning to let God be God, and to not allow my confusion to be the focus of our relationship anymore."[5]

This shift of allowing God to be God was what moved Strahan into a hugely different relationship with Him. Instead of bartering, bargaining, and praying perfect prayers, he began to wait with God. "I was learning that the greatest power in prayer is to *be* together with God and that being is often as much the answer to the prayers we're praying as the answers we're seeking themselves."

Silence in waiting

As I shared earlier, my husband and I refer to a really bad day as our "being eaten by the bear." We've all experienced days like those. Sometimes, waiting on God lasts more than a day. It can even stretch into years. It is not based on our lack of faith or maturity. Waiting on God is something that all believers experience. It is not *if* waiting will happen. It is *when* it happens. Our waiting does not have a clear ending. The indefinite time required can cause stress itself and that stress can feel like an attack. "How long, God? How long?" is a universally understood question. (See Psalm 13:1-2)

We each wrestle with a different "bear." Maybe for you, it's ongoing physical pain. Maybe it's relational brokenness. Or loneliness. Or financial struggles. You keep praying, but the bear keeps attacking, and God seems far away. What is the dream you have been praying for that has not been realized? Is it the prodigal son or daughter who has turned their back on you, as well as on the Lord? Or is it a disease that was healed but has returned? It's in times such as these that we need an answer from the Lord who just in speaking would restore our peace. But what we receive as we wait on God is more than the answers to our prayers.

All of us want the ability to trust God's goodness in the waiting when He is silent. When we seek clarity, we can find mystery instead. When we cry out to Him for a cure, deliverance, healing, but things remain the same, what is our response? Do we accept it as our spiritual cross to bear or our lack of faith? If our trust is not built in these testy times of waiting, then it can erode our faith. Doubt can jab at our faith in the God we love and desperately need.

In his book *Praying Like Monks, Living Like Fools*, Tyler Staton shares the story of Jenna, a close friend who had gone through incredible trauma and hardship. Though impoverished, she chose to care for her dying sister and her infant nephew. As she fervently prayed for her sister to recover, she was met with silence. "If God responded with a straightforward no, it'd be a bitter pill, but at least we'd know God heard us and in his infinite wisdom and eternal perspective responded in the negative. But silence? Silence feels like apathy for the sufferer, like God is unmoved and uncaring about what's going on down here."[6]

In times of silence, our worst fears can threaten. We might think God has deserted us. In that place of discouragement, we have a choice. To try to ride out the feelings, like it's just a bad day. Or we can fight with weapons that are not of this world. In that place of harrowing silence, we can choose the truth of scripture that begs to differ with our doubts. God's words are the truth that slays the enemy's lies, that enables us to be resilient.

When God is silent, the enemy's attacks can fuel our feelings of abandonment. But if I turn to the sword of the Spirit, the Word of God, His offensive weapon will cut across the lies and bring truth. "For the word of God is living and active, sharper than a two-edged sword, piercing even to the division of soul and of spirit, of joints and of marrow, and discerning the thoughts and intentions of the heart." (Hebrews 4:12, ESV), God's Word tells us the truth about His character. He will never leave us or forsake us. (See Deuteronomy 31:8, Hebrews 13:5) He cares for us as a Father cares for His children. (See Psalm 103:13, 2 Corinthians 6:18)

The power of praying friends

When the waiting gets its hardest, reaching out to praying friends can make all the difference. The Lord tells us that the prayers of the righteous are effective. James 5:16 reminds us of this truth: "The prayer of a righteous person has great power as it is working." When my prayers lack energy or substance, I call or text those closest to me. When there is an outright emergency, they have my back. In the same way I am there for them.

There are friends who have been there for each other, supporting one another, for thirty-some-odd years. We share the same "I need help" prayer privilege with each other. When we say we need prayer, our names are lifted to the Lord immediately. For us, prayer is serious business. We have rocked babies while we have prayed together for healing. We have gotten babysitters to free us up for prayer when it has meant the difference between life and death. We were there at 3 a.m., when we were awakened at the same time on different sides of the continent. We have prayed for prodigal children, our husbands' heart attacks, and finding homes. We praised God collectively as He brought salvation, healing and guided us forward. One friend has a handicapped child, and another has a husband with physical challenges. One is raising grandchildren while another consistently feeds a newborn so the mother can sleep. All the while, prayers are lifted up for each other's requests. Despite the hurdles to prayer, their lives are filled with regular sessions and the constant up-lifting of heart-felt needs, depositing them into the hands of God.

One of the longest-held prayers was for a friend's grown daughter bound in the grips of domestic violence. The court kept our friend's grandchild in a cycle of shared supervision with the other grandparents whose home was filled with anger, addiction, and persistent threats against her daughter. As her case wound from family court to criminal court, in two states, we prayed. After five years, the courts finally granted my friend custody of her grandchild. Waiting on the Lord not only helped to strengthen our faith, it helped to keep peace for my friend through each legal step as it unfolded. Our prayers provided a bridge that kept us focused on the Lord when it would've been easier to give up. God turned things around for this family while they waited on Him to act. Faithful prayers connected them to God's power and love when their faith and finances were running low. Prayers were the pathways He used to move on their behalf.

We've all been there, haven't we? "How long, O Lord? Will you forget me forever?" Psalm 13:1 echoes those feelings. But read further. Psalm 16:8: "I have set the Lord always before me. Because He is at my right hand, I will not be shaken." (ESV) The truth is we are not forgotten. Silent or speaking to you, God has committed to always be with you. "The Lord Himself goes before you and will be with you; He will never leave you and forsake you. Do not be afraid; do not be discouraged." (Deuteronomy 31:8) In the silence, when you are seeking Him and hearing nothing, bare your heart to Him and rest in that silence. He is there. He is with you. This is where you will find His sustaining strength. You will move from fear to faith as He provides Himself in the silence. Just because God is silent does not mean He is distant. Use the times that He seems silent to meet Him in the silence, rest there, and listen.

We will all experience seasons, long or short, when the answer is not yes or no. His answer is to wait. But as we shift our attention away from the problem and on to the Lord, waiting becomes a vehicle for spiritual change. Waiting on God builds the discipline of patience. In the waiting, as we cling to Him despite our feelings or needs, He gives us Himself.

The power of persistence

We connect to God through prayer. It is a lifeline when we are in a dry, waiting season. Through prayer we access strength from the Lord to keep going. Recently, as I read Luke 18:1-8 about the persistent widow, I received new insight on the connection between persistence and faith. Hang with me as we unpack this parable.

Jesus tells us what the parable is about. It is "to show them (us) that they should always pray and not give up." Several versions read "pray and not lose heart." If we can hold onto God when we wait, we position ourselves to grow. It is the fertile ground for what He wants to grow in us. Persistence and resilience unite in growing our character and our faith.

Jesus introduces a hard-hearted judge who would not be moved by a widow's plea for justice. But over time, because of her persistence, he is moved to act. She did not lose heart. Jesus is using this story to provide a roadmap for faith. He is instructing us to hold onto Him when things don't change; that we "should always pray and not give up." There is something key in our *continuing* to pray. What we ask for isn't less important. But continuing to hold onto Him allows persistence, perseverance, and endurance to be formed in us.

Then Jesus ends this story with a stunning question. "When the Son of Man comes, will He find faith on the earth?" (Luke 18:8) He is speaking to you and me. Will our waiting on Him continue in faith? Will we continue to hold on to God during extreme hardship? Will our faith be proved as we hold fast to God in prayer? As we continue to hold on and not lose heart, we are walking in the faith that God is supplying.

I wondered as I read the passage, is this parable not only about persistence in prayer, but is Jesus telling us how faith is formed? Is this the evidence of faith as the Bible describes in Hebrews 11:1: "Now faith is the substance of things hoped for, and the evidence of things not seen." (NKJV) Could we demonstrate faith in the days leading up to His coming as we hold fast to Him? Could persistent prayer build faith? When God asks us to wait, is He also enlarging our capacity to build faith? Could one of the functions of prayer be to receive strength from God as we hold on? Could Jesus be telling us to be faithful as we hold on in persistently praying? Sounds counter-intuitive, doesn't it? Who gains strength while continuing to pray when there hasn't been an answer? Those that wait on the Lord.

"Those who wait on the Lord will renew their strength. They will mount up with wings like eagles; they will run and not be weary. They will walk and not faint." (Isaiah 40:31, NKJV). The chorus that I have sung following that verse continues with, "Teach me, Lord. Teach me, Lord, how to wait."

We do not wear out God with our pleas for justice. Our asking Him to remove adversity and its effects do not put Him off. But God has a larger purpose in our waiting. Just as there's a process being built into the widow in this parable, there is faith being built in us as we are persistent.

As we pray, our faith stretches and grows as we persist. My faith is made stronger if I continue to hold onto Him in prayer. My waiting on God to act forms a resistance of sorts to my faith muscles. These muscles increase with the resistance in waiting. I persist and my faith increases. In persistence He provides the fuel, energy, and provision for my faith if I will stay the course with Him. My faith increases and then there's a bonus: my trust in God grows and flourishes!

When healing doesn't happen

In living with depression, I maintain a place of hope for change, for God's best in this body and mind. I continue to pray for steps forward that bring His life to me. When I need to cancel a meeting with friends, bow out of a commitment to serve, or delay a project that has a deadline, I receive His grace that in time brings me hope. His will is filled with grace and love. He will bring grace and love through and despite this condition. He even brings purpose and gives me grace when I cannot give it to myself. When I submit to His will, though it may not look like his perfect will, I am submitting to Him. My hope is found in accepting His way through.

Offenses, complications, weariness, disconnection, isolation, and confusion can deplete our faith. God's plan is that the hardship of waiting for an answer in these situations would be used for our good. When the Apostle Paul prayed for relief from suffering, God's response was, "'My grace is sufficient for you, for my power is made perfect in weakness.'" Paul's take-away was: "Therefore I will boast all the more gladly about my weaknesses, so that Christ's power may rest on me." (2 Corinthians 12: 9)

Our best intentions, right answers to problems, or hope for healed disease may not happen. But the time spent waiting on Him, accepting His way through, and His answers to these situations, will bring His strength to us.

The weaknesses you see in yourself are the places God will provide strength as you ask. Do not let your impatience in the waiting for answers bring bitterness. Do not let waiting on God become a source of discouragement. Stay connected to Him in the middle of it all. Pray your heart and hear His. Your persistent prayers will be His pipeline for Him providing strength.

Resilience comes as He takes those painful circumstances that persist and not only heals you but also makes you even stronger than you were prior to the struggle. He provides Himself as your answer. He will give you the way to move forward with a more resilient faith.

Resting as we wait

When I was in college, I earned my Life Saving Certificate, which would allow me to work as a lifeguard during the summers and save money for the next college semester. During that course we had to prove we could "survival float" in the water, fully clothed, shoes on, for thirty minutes. My legs and arms would dangle with my face in the water until I needed air. Then in jellyfish-fashion, I quickly pulled my arms toward my torso and pulled my legs together. I would lift my head to the water's surface and fill my lungs with air, then return to the dangling position. The secret of survival floating was to stay relaxed at all times. If I became anxious, my body would automatically tighten and weigh me down. I learned that the tension in our muscles creates weight and works to restrict our ability to float. So, the secret is to rest in the water and just relax. You can go on and on if you rest. You get the parallel, right?

Perseverance in prayer works on the same principle. We need to rest and relax while we wait. If we are resting in our dangling position as we pray and persist, we can trust Him in the process of waiting. If we become anxious about the outcome or use our own strength to persevere, we won't be able to go the distance. Keeping our focus on the Lord and using our weakness as a place of receiving from Him are the hallmarks of persistent waiting. As we wait on Him in prayer, we gain strength, grow our faith, and prove our trust in Him.

Faith does not change depending on the conditions around us. No matter if our circumstances are bleak, the struggle is on-going, or the healing hasn't happened, God is the same. Faith is operating in us whether we see answers or not. The truth of God's Word is the same no matter the details of your life or mine. The truth of walking by faith is operating no matter the current circumstances we experience. Faith for those of us with physical or emotional limitations works the same as for those without them.

I'm asking God that as you pray without ceasing, He will continue to form and strengthen resilient faith in you. That you would be strengthened through difficulty, grow stronger as you are challenged. That you go from strength to strength in your faith.

Believing for change

You may be wondering how the principles of growth mindset and possibility-thinking apply to people with physical limitations. If difficulties are extreme, do we set aside our faith and our growth? Could growth mindset principles operate in situations where there are persistent emotional limitations? When people have mental or physical limitations they still need to grow, learn, and achieve. The possibility-thinking in a growth mindset works just as well with people that have disabilities. Growth mindset principles function the same way no matter what the limitations are. They are, however, applied in a modified way as compared to someone without limitations.

Let's look at how that works. My lifelong friend is the caregiver and mom to an adult handicapped son. Her responsibilities as a caregiver include goal setting and assessing those goals. She will modify the goals that have not been achieved and break those down into more attainable steps for the next period. Once the goal is reached, she develops another one within his skill level that requires a little more effort from her son. She has goals for his physical, mental and emotional well-being. His resilience determines how much he is willing to attempt at any given time. Although there are things he cannot accomplish, goal setting keeps him focused on the areas that are within his realm of possibility. This process helps him to see his progress even when it is small. Focusing on what is doable is the foundation of maintaining a growth mindset for his situation.

How can people move forward when accidents happen, illnesses are not healed, or when they have physical or mental limitations? How can they grow and maintain their faith? The same way we all do, one step at a time, one day at a time. They consider what is possible, take small steps and believe that the efforts that they are making are actual accomplishments worthy of celebrating. The possibility-thinking in growth mindset we read about in the last chapter applies to those of us with physical and mental issues as well as those without those issues. The strategies are just applied differently and modified to fit the person's abilities.

I make sure to safeguard my thinking during a depressive episode by not tackling too many tasks. When I am tired because anxiety keeps me from sleeping, I give myself grace, but I don't give-in to self-doubt. I allow for extra comfort, down time and practice patience, giving myself grace. I expect less of myself during those times. I read, journal, do light exercise and pray. It may be several days before real strides toward feeling better happen, but I don't want my attitude to be one of giving up. Good days will come again. But while there's depression, I am investing in my faith by focusing on God's goodness and a change that hasn't happened *yet*.

Choose to believe the truth

I tag the depression as a bear, but it doesn't eat me every day. For that I am grateful. And even when it feels like the depression is going to devour me, I have choices. I pause in the pressure of depression to take hold of Jesus. He is there with me, whenever the feelings of hopelessness close in. At my weakest moments, lies confront me. They mockingly say if God really loved me He would heal me. The lies scream that I will be broken beyond repair and God will not shield me from it happening. I make a choice not to believe the lies of negativity and condemnation that the enemy challenges and chastises me with. Instead, I confront those lies with the truth: "Therefore, there is now no condemnation for those who are in Christ Jesus, because through Christ Jesus the law of the Spirit who gives life has set you free from the law of sin and death." (Romans 8:1-2) I can choose to state the truth that God has given me.

My favorite verse in the battle between truth and lies is 2

Corinthians 10:5: I "take captive every thought to make it obedient to Christ." By doing what this verse says I am taking the Word of God and wearing it around me as a breastplate. I can demolish lies with the truth (Ephesians 6:14-17). Then I rest beneath the shadow of His wings (Psalm 91:1). What that means for me is that any time depression raises its head, I have a deliverer. He takes charge of that battle. I keep in mind that the battle is the Lord's, (1 Samuel 7:47) but we are in this together. He stands guard over me, but I need to do practical things in my waiting to stabilize my mind and secure my emotions.

I am writing these words of encouragement as fighting words for us all. Keep your hope in the Lord before you as you wait. Rest in Him in that hope. If you are being confronted as you read this, know that He is your hope. Remember, the Lord is a rewarder of those that diligently seek Him and in Him is the reward!

"But without faith it is impossible to please Him, for he who comes to God must believe that He is, and that He is a rewarder of those who diligently seek Him." (Hebrews 11:6, NKJV) As we lean into Him and depend on His help, we are actively walking by faith.

Unanswered questions and unresolved issues are opportunities to grow faith. We are committing to press into His ever-prevailing strength as He sustains us through every trauma and hardship. Any adversity brings with it the paradox of pain. When I face pain, I can fight it myself or I can ask God to walk with me in it and then fight it together. I can ask Him to make this adverse situation the vessel He would use to take me deeper into His grace and mercy.

We all know He answers prayer, but sometimes it doesn't happen when we want it to. Whether it was cancer, depression, or a child that lost their way, by not having a quick answer, a miracle healing, or the next step, a different kind answer came instead. Because of waiting, I grew closer to Him. I leaned into His strength. He reassured me of better things to come. He promised His will would bring greater glory to Him. And I have to say, that is true. The answers weren't what I wanted, but the benefits were beyond what I could've imagined. In the season of waiting on answers, we have God.

The difficulty and tension of navigating through waiting can offer an opportunity to know Him in a way that you simply could not get in any other way. It is an offering, a gift. You are giving God the gift of a surrendered heart. He sees and He receives you there. You are not alone in the waiting. God is with you. As you move through this together, God is building resilience in you. He allows you to create space for faith to grow.

In fighting both the bear of depression and recurrent thyroid cancer, I have learned to war with spiritual weapons of faith, hope, and truth of His Word, and to worship no matter what. I have learned that to fall down in that battle is to fall on Him. In my weakness, He is my strength. God works all things together for my good. He works all things together for your good. Through our struggles we are being given access to His strength. His strength prevails.

Psalm 59:16 assures us: "But I will sing of your strength, in the morning I will sing of your love for you are my fortress, my refuge in times of trouble." Go deep with the Lord as you wait. Trust Him as your focus as you wait. You are waiting on *His* timing. Your hope is in God. He will not fail you.

TAKEAWAYS

- What we receive as we wait on God is more than the answers to our prayers.
- God uses seasons of waiting with Him as a vehicle to build trust, hope, and faith.
- Because God is silent does not mean He is distant. Use the times that He seems silent to meet Him in the silence, rest there, and listen.
- The prayer of relinquishment can be used as one way to let go of control and surrender to His will.

SPIRITUAL PRACTICE: THE PRAYER OF RELINQUISHMENT

Relinquishing our desires to God is foundational in learning how to wait on God. The prayer of relinquishment can be tailored to your circumstances and used to declare that He is the creator of life and our guide in how we live ours. It is an act of letting go of trying to control our situation and putting our needs into God's hands.

In your own words, confess the ways you have attempted to control your life. Then surrender to His will. Ask God to show you a more excellent way to pray through the waiting. If He shows you that, take it as your next step. Simple surrender is beautiful to Him. Thank Him for the way He is leading you!

CHAPTER 4

Combating Crisis Fatigue

My grace is sufficient for you, for my power is made perfect in
weakness.

–2 Corinthians 12:9, ESV

SHARP, cutting pain, like fire, incessantly burned a streak from
underneath my left arm to my fingers. The doctor poked my underarm,
patted my chest where the mastectomy had left its marks, then stood
back and thought. "It might be multiple sclerosis. We'll get you to a
neurologist and they will run a battery of tests."

"But the pain?"

"Sounds like nerve involvement. We've got meds that will help."

My mind raced to the next steps. I shook my head. Would I have to
go to another specialist for more tests? An orthopedic specialist, an
endocrinologist, and a rheumatologist had filled the last month with
scans, procedures, and speculation. During that same time, I had gone
to my chiropractor, a massage therapist, and had long sessions of
prayer for relief. I had asked the Lord for His leading, His insight, and
a rock we hadn't looked under. Nothing was turning up answers. One
specialist referred me to another specialist and the whole routine

would begin again. The pain continued, its burning streaks telling my body and any specialist who would listen that there was trouble here.

When there's physical pain, there's emotional suffering. Anyone who deals with on-going pain finds themselves on a path that can seem to lead nowhere. I searched for solutions that were hard to find. I reluctantly agreed to medications only to have unbearable side effects. I tried therapies that offered to short-circuit the pain, finding temporary relief. Then, without any warning or reason, the sharp pain returned with a vengeance. Without answers the suffering pushed away my logic. I needed help. I set aside my doubts in the system and started with a new neurologist, an orthopedic specialist and a naturopath. I repeated the scenario with new doctors who offered new suggestions, while I hoped for a different outcome. I was exhausted. As it continued, my search for the cause of pain took second place to wanting relief. Just one moment without pain. That's all I was asking for.

Electrical currents pulsed down my arm day and night, and I began to believe that the pain would overtake my life. Though it would stop for a moment or two, it would start again as if it were on a looping cycle. I couldn't sleep, rest, or relax. If I distracted myself with activity, it was just a diversion. It would remind me that a brief interlude was just a commercial break, not a remedy. The pain was in charge. I was not.

The doctors called it intermittent and aggressive. Intermittent because it sent pulses down my arm and aggressive because it was just that. The pain was the boss of me. Where I went and what I did was ruled by the aggressor. I rated it a nine out of ten on the familiar scale of pain ratings. It was always there.

Going through a prophetic passage

As the struggle continued, I sought relief in medicine, therapies, and nutrition. I wanted my mind sharp, so I stayed away from pain killers and attempted to keep a schedule with work and family. I regularly received prayer in our home group, with friends and at church.

Often, I had to step out of activities. But when my husband proposed I travel with him on a business trip to Montana, I agreed. At this point, the nerve medication had brought some relief. Because of this, I thought it might be a healthy distraction from the cycle of seeing doctors, getting tests, and waiting for a diagnosis. Montana was more than a diversion; it was a bucket list goal. We had two days before his meetings started and headed to Glacier National Park with hopes of traversing the Going to the Sun Pass. What we couldn't have known is that the spring thaw was running behind its seasonal schedule.

We pulled up to the ranger's headquarters just in time to learn we would be the first car to go through the Pass. There we were, wide-eyed and ready, our rental car poised right behind the snowplow with a line of cars behind us. The snow was still thick as the snowplow plodded up the mountain, slowly clearing the way as we headed up the narrow passage right behind. The tension in the car was as thick as the fog. I prayed and watched as the edge of the road appeared and then disappeared right along with the plow in a swath of thick clouds. Could my husband drive when he couldn't see the road? Soon we were not sure if we were following right behind the snowplow or if it was miles ahead of us. As we gained altitude, the fog combined with snow clouds. Visibility zero.

I nestled the bag of frozen peas I had brought between my left arm and my chest like a life preserver. It cooled the recurring bursts of pain. But as the temperature dropped and we struggled to keep up with the snowplow, my nerves, and the peas, chilled me to the bone. My teeth chattered. I held the passenger door handle tightly, as though it could save me. I prayed that my husband could keep the car on the road without actually seeing it. I prayed the packed snow wouldn't create infamous layers of black ice. Clouds would periodically thin, so I dared to look over the edge at thousands of feet below. Deep thick forests and mountainous terrain stared back.

"Keep your eyes on the road, hon. Try to stay right behind him!"

"I am. I am." His shoulders were erect, and his hands gripped the steering wheel tightly at 10 and 2.

Every mile or so a gentle waterfall would spring up, running down the mountain, cascading over the road and heading down the opposite edge of the embankment.

"Keep your eyes on the snowplow, Charlie." I was talking to myself as well as encouraging him. I couldn't help myself.

Soon the majesty of the views competed with the sheer terror of the conditions. Through short breaks in the fog, a startling glimpse of the deep blue Montana sky appeared. The mountain stretched higher and higher. Cars followed behind us and we fought to stay within sight of the snowplow. Finally, after close to an hour of slow climbing, we began the descent. We had navigated through the Pass.

As slowly as the snowpacks had increased on the way up, they began to dissolve as we headed down the other side of the mountain. Dark green swathes of forest and cerulean, blue sky illuminated the view. Finally, the snow flurries gave way to crystal clear skies and a vista that escaped description. Peaks of granite, aqua colored mountain lakes, emerald forests spread out before us as far as we could see.

Just as we made our way through the pass and down the other side of the mountain, a lone bicycle rider approached us. His handlebar mustache was frozen, and his face flushed red with exertion as he climbed up the mountain. His bike was evenly balanced with packs on either side of the back wheels. He would face the fog, snow, and challenging incline we had just experienced. But he wouldn't have the protection of a windshield or a snowplow leading the way. I steadied my phone, snapping a quick picture as we laughed thinking about his audacity. Then just as I reached down to put my phone back in my purse, I heard the Lord say, "This is the journey you are getting ready to take."

Instantly, I identified with the cyclist and the treacherous circumstances before him. He was heading into zero visibility and freezing temperatures. Wind, ice, and snow waited for him as he navigated the Pass. I wondered about the danger of my situation, but I felt a strange new sense of peace. Hearing God's voice diffused my fear. His voice brought clarity and steeled my resolve to keep my eyes on Him much like we had with the snowplow. I repeated His words. After all these months of wondering, the voice of God clearly told me that this cyclist was a picture of what lay ahead for me.

When I got home, I printed the picture of the lone cyclist. Frozen, intense, and determined, his image was prophetic, motivating me to set my intentions before I knew what I faced. I knew I would never be able to pedal up the Rocky Mountains. But what I could do was follow the Lord daily, taking small steps with the same focused determination that the cyclist displayed. I put magnets around the picture and studied his face as I secured it to the refrigerator door. His picture reminded me that the Lord is with me, and He wants me to know that He knows the way through.

Because of the Going to the Sun passage experience, I had a sense of being prepared for battle. The pain was still there, but I knew that the Lord was leading the way. The Lord knew the direction I needed to take, and He was showing me that I would come through it. He was telling me how to fix my heart, mind, and body on Him with greater perseverance and determination than I had known. Just like the cyclist I had prepared myself with packs of every imaginable provision. I fueled my heart and mind daily. I rested in His presence. I tried not to wonder about the future but kept my mind on the present. The journey was going to be challenging, but the Lord knew the way through. A mountainous battle lay before me, but my life and my future were in God's hands.

Psalm 18:32-34 says: "It is God who arms me with strength and keeps my way secure. He makes my feet like the feet of a deer; he causes me to stand on the heights. He trains my hands for battle; my arms can bend a bow of bronze." We would head up the mountain together and He would make the way sure and certain.

Through the Lord's insight, I had a sense of what the coming months would be like. Just like the fog and the clouds hid the road ahead of us, I would not walk by sight. There would be great challenges and extreme circumstances. But I was committed to staying close to Him, just as we had determined to stay close behind the snowplow. I would make it through, even as I was certain that the cyclist had made it through. I would hold on to God's prophetic insight. God was making a way to pass through my "Going to the Son" Pass. He would enable me to stand on the heights with Him. It would be bone chilling, and I might face narrow passages. But I was determined to hold onto Him no matter what.

A song from the Lord

During the months that I sought a diagnosis, we faced multiple crises as a family. One of our grown children suffered from a debilitating condition. The twins were both planning for college admission and needed support with applications and finances. Then as I went to get an MRI to narrow the field of diagnostic possibilities, I located a hitch in our medical insurance. At this point I was weak physically and spiritually. I was running low on strength and courage.

My first MRI found nothing in my arm or shoulder. If I were to receive the second one that I insisted on having, I would need to pay cash. But I felt strongly it was the only way to move forward. We had investigated every other medical lead. All of which led nowhere. This was the last chance.

A month later, I walked into the MRI unit and told the technicians the problem. "Please move the frames on the scan as far out as possible. I need to find something that was undetected in the first scan." They nodded in agreement.

Within days, the results were in and my oncologist from fifteen years earlier called for an appointment. "We have an answer. Your breast cancer has returned. To stage it we need you to get a PET scan." I had no response. I had waited and wanted a diagnosis. Now it was here. The mountain was in front of me. Now it was time to climb that mountain with the Lord.

This was cancer number three. The first breast cancer was diagnosed fourteen years earlier. The Lord had told me then that I would live and not die. He had kept me alive during the ups and downs of thyroid cancer four years earlier, including the frightening severe anaphylactic reaction to the nuclear iodine treatment. But He had made a way. Was there a time limit to that original promise of life? "I will not die but live, and will proclaim what the Lord has done." Psalm 118:17 Did that promise have a time stamp on it? Did it expire after I lived through the first cancer? Or could that promise mean I would live through this one as I had with the second cancer?

The day for the PET scan results had arrived. I waited for a ride to the appointment and my mind raced. The results would tell the ultimate story. It would show any other tumors anywhere in my body within two centimeters in size. Would there be cancer that had traveled to major organs? Would it prove that my days were numbered and that those numbers were few? My emotions were all over the place as I prayed for calm and steadiness.

Suddenly a melody began repeating itself inside my head. It was something I had never heard before. It repeated again and again. The Holy Spirit was singing to me. It was a beautiful melody. Does it have words? I wondered if I could locate it in the old *Broadman Hymnal* I had. But how could I look for it by only hearing a melody? It repeated. I got the old green hymnal and flipped it to the back where the first lines of the hymns were listed in alphabetical order. Just then the first line came to me, "Be still my soul, the Lord is on your side." I had never heard it before. I was certain of that. But now I had heard it. The Holy Spirit was singing a melody to me, and I heard it for the first time. He was singing a hymn, and I needed those words!

I sang with the melody and the words as I read through them.

"Be still my soul. The Lord is on your side.
Bear patiently the cross of grief or pain.
Leave to thy God to order and provide
In every change He faithful will remain."[1]

Tears streamed down my cheeks as I sang through the stanzas. The Lord was making certain that His love enveloped me as I went to hear the PET results. No matter what that scan showed, I was not going there alone. He was with me and on my side.

I was still afraid of the scan results. I still had questions. I felt I needed answers about what was next. I wanted to know that I would live, for one. I still had to face those details and deal with the reality of cancer treatments and pain. But at the same time, the exact same time, hearing the Lord tell me He is with me brought peace like a river. It buoyed me up with hope. He was with me, and He had made sure that I knew it. His peace would be with me. I could trust Him to do what He said He would do. I still had shaky knees. But deeper, in my core, God held me.

It's not the miraculous details that hold you and I. It's the hope and security that His presence brings. He is with you in your greatest need. He may not answer your questions, but He wants to hear them from you. Much like the song that He sang to me, He will give you answers that you could not have seen coming.

A mountainous battle

After the PET scan, I was again in my doctor's office. Dr. M. put the file next to me on the examining table and grimaced. I had been one of his first patients in his oncology practice fifteen years ago, when I first was diagnosed with breast cancer. He was empathic, straightforward and tough. He got eye to eye with me, and I swallowed hard.

"The rate for survival for women with distant metastatic breast cancer is 29 percent," he said. "But about one-third of the women diagnosed with MBC in the U.S. live at least five years after diagnosis. Some live ten or more years." Then he told me the truth I would latch onto: "You can beat this!"

The pain that burned up and down my left arm was not multiple sclerosis or nerve pain. It was the dragon I thought I'd slain ten years before. The burning that had continued for months was pointing us to a tumor the size of a baseball that was growing into a nerve in the quiet corner of my brachial plexus. Dr. M. diagnosed me with Stage IV breast cancer that day. I was 55 years old.

Digesting the odds of surviving cancer felt like peering down the barrel of a loaded shotgun. But something dawned on me. The statistics produced were from the combined averages of all women with Stage IV breast cancer. They did not reflect the chances of a single individual's physical ability to survive the disease. I was not a statistic to God. He'd brought me through cancer twice before. Just how resilient was my faith in Him to face it now?

God had a hand in my survival just as He had with each woman I sat with in the radiation clinic waiting areas. I held hands with them in prayer groups. I shared fears and dreams with them over coffee. Whether they were thirty or seventy-seven years old, none of them were willing to become part of the seventy-one percent that succumbed to this disease. These odds sounded overwhelming. But I wondered, could they also be a call to action? I was sobered by the statistics. But at the same time, I asked God for mercy. Could I follow hard after Him and see a different outcome?

That summer I received thirty-six radiation doses for two areas of breast cancer. At times they caused pain, and then toward the end formed blisters on my skin. My body felt like I had swallowed the Olympic flame. I was burning from the inside out. But during each session on that radiation table, I would envision the Lord's hand healing and restoring my body. The Lord kept me in perfect peace as I waited in stillness for each dose.

It had been a summer of miracles. The Lord had navigated my way through Stage IV breast cancer. It was very similar to passing through a shrouded mountain pass. What had started with sharp, slicing pain ended with blisters from radiation, minor scars, and a silent awe of His ways. The electric surges of pain in my arm had been necessary. They had screamed for attention and showed the doctors what was still growing in my body. It was an alarm that kept us searching for the cause. Through it, God was teaching me how to hold fast, to keep my eyes on Him and keep going, despite the battle. Through it all, I was participating in the unfolding of a miracle.

Crisis fatigue

I want to look at the connection between physical suffering and the layered suffering of continuous adversity. Even when the problems are circumstantial and not originating in our bodies, it causes physical suffering. When we suffer, when there's stress, or when we are severely impacted by on-going difficulties, research confirms that our bodies' functions are altered. "Long term stress leaves us at risk of developing health conditions such as diabetes, high blood pressure and obesity," Hilda Burke, author and therapist writes. She continues with a step to take. "Changing our mindset and actively working with what we have control of in our lives can limit the effects."[2]

The world we live in is filled with natural disasters, social pressures, and personal hardships. The phenomena of crisis fatigue results when one tragic event happens alongside another. Sometimes they are simultaneous. In the case of natural disasters, such as hurricanes that strip communities of support systems, people may lose a home, family members and not have a community to depend on. Multiple adverse events occur when a family member is diagnosed with a disease, making them unable to work, resulting in financial and health concerns.

What we have come to know as crisis fatigue is used to describe chronic stress and fatigue, which stems from prolonged conflict or adversity. When this happens, the resulting stress that accompanies it seems to continue as if in overdrive. Recent examples include ongoing wars, wildfires, powerful storms, and mass shootings. The truth is that people are not equipped to stay focused on ongoing or traumatic occurrences. Compounding events or ones that continue can lead to depression, anxiety, and swings in sleep patterns such as oversleeping or insomnia. When a crisis is ongoing, people can retreat and isolate, lose interest in living, and let go of relationships.

"This (crisis fatigue) is not a clinically diagnosed condition," said Dr. Harold Levine, chief medical officer for BayCare Behavioral Health. "However, given the challenges we've faced in the last few years, people are experiencing high levels of chronic stress, anxiety, depression, and hopelessness."[3]

Our ability to build resilience is a major safeguard against the symptoms of crisis fatigue. Having faith in God's ability to strengthen us and undergird us in times of intense adversity is the first and best defense for dealing with the stress that accompanies crisis no matter how layered it is. Having our focus on His provision in such times sustains our hope and defeats hopelessness. Instead of being perpetually distracted by war and the destruction released by earthquakes or mega-powerful storms, we fix our eyes on God's help, praying into the areas that need support.

Having faith in God's ability to strengthen us and undergird us in times of intense adversity is the first and best defense for dealing with the stress that accompanies crisis no matter how layered it is.

That switch in perspective can begin to build resilience and create a mindset against the fallout of continuous or multilayered adversity. Moving from hopelessness to hope in God's ability to support and bring us help settles our hearts. Hoping in Him serves as a grounding mechanism. Shifting towards Him can serve to secure our hearts and minds. As Hebrews 6:19 says, "We have this hope as an anchor for the soul, firm and secure." Fixing our mind on God offers us that secured anchor.

How we make it through

When my diagnosis occurred, both of our extended families were miles away. But compassionate people from our church took care of the details. God made a way using generous people as His hands and feet. He brought friends with the gift of laughter, rides to appointments when I couldn't drive, and intervened with the always-welcomed casserole just when our family needed them most. People served us with double helpings of hope, encouragement, and demonstrations of His love. When I was down, a simple gift of hand-picked wildflowers lifted my spirit. At times, a friend mentioning a forgotten memory on a hand-written card offered tangible hope. I knew God was caring for my family through these acts of love. He used my struggles to form a deeper bond in our community. He used the difficulties we faced to show me how to give to others.

During the summer of 2005, I filled a hard-bound navy journal with pencil sketches, letters to Jesus, and watercolor landscapes that framed encouraging phrases. I listed dreams of what I could do next summer, like go to the top of the Eiffel Tower; people I wanted to visit, like my hilarious Uncle Raymond; and if-only activities I could plan, like trips to the mountains with my besties. Journaling had been a life-long way to process with the Lord; to record the verses He supported me with and document my spiritual journey. But that summer, it reflected my hopes and aspirations. The journal housed my goals and intentions for after radiation treatments. The heavier-stock pages kept the colors from running when tears dotted the page and kept them from seeping into yesterday's entry. God used the simple journal sessions to draw my focus to the future. Even as I grieved I did it in light of the hope I had in Him.

The self-care practices I used that kept me restored physically and emotionally were those that were most accessible at the time. I didn't need to use bath bombs or expensive oils. A twenty-minute soak in an Epsom salt bath, watching the sun set, or reading Mary Oliver poetry eased my mind and my muscles. Going to bed at ten, enjoying a blue-berry smoothie, and walking long distances on nature trails were necessary physical routines that supported my mental wellbeing. They prepared me for the strenuous mental, emotional, and spiritual chal-lenges I would face in recuperating after radiation. When you are dealing with disease, you can practice nutritional and self-care routines that keep your body supported while it heals.

The spiritual changes I needed to make soon became clear. God began to remind me that He had not created me to be a racehorse (His analogy). I might be able to check-off my to-do list by noon, but the stress that pace created cost me. When I stopped to think about the point He was trying to get across, I realized He was weaving grace into my worn-out body and my soul. What He offered instead was a slower pace and peace so that each day could be enjoyed. Instead of pushing myself when I was tired, I reminded myself to take breaks. If I paused throughout the day to be mindful of His care, He would use that pause to provide me with peace. If I asked for His approach to a given situation, instead of rushing through it, there seemed to be time and energy at the end of the day.

Slowing down became a spiritual practice. The Lord led me to let go of the way I took hold of life. No more racehorse. I had to surrender my get-it-done mentality for an unfamiliar, turtle-like pace. The Lord taught me to be mindful of how I did what I did; to be aware of my urgency, my need for speed. He had a pace and wanted me to follow Him in it. "Take a deep breath. What's the hurry? Why wear yourself out? Just what are you after anyway?" (Jeremiah 2:25, MSG)

Doing our part

We don't know what life will bring our way. We stay equipped for challenging seasons by keeping our body, mind, and soul healthy on those less challenging days. It is the practical and everyday routines that work like an investment preparing us to go through any crisis.

When I say healthy, I mean I am focused on doing my part to take care of this earthly temple. I faced a disease that required extra care in many ways: staying on top of dosing medications, recording side effects, and even taking regular blood pressure readings. But the critical part I played was to maintain my body the way I always had. I made sure my high protein smoothie offered everything my body needed regardless of the medications. As I held fast to God, I took daily walks, wrote in my journal, and at the end of the day, kicked back for a long laugh with a friend. In a lengthy battle, being consistent to take care of ourselves is crucial. By continuing to take care of myself, I was unconsciously telling my body: "everything is going to be alright."

Tish Harrison Warren, in *Liturgy of the Ordinary: Sacred Practices in Everyday Life*, writes: "Everyone wants a revolution, but nobody wants to do the dishes." She continues, "I often want to skip the boring, daily stuff to get to the thrill of an edgy faith. But it's in the dailiness of the Christian faith--the making the bed, the doing the dishes, the praying for our enemies, the reading the Bible, the quiet, the small—that God's transformation takes root and grows."[4]

We may think that our miraculous breakthrough is going to come in a bolt of anointing aimed precisely at our adversity. But God is working to will His good pleasure in our routine, everyday, ordinary lives.

Changing our mindset and actively working with what we can control in our lives can limit the effects of an ongoing crisis.

Changing our mindset and actively working with what we can control in our lives can limit the effects of an ongoing crisis. When we take walks, appreciate the beauty of nature, or absorb the encouragement and comfort found in the Psalm, we are taking responsibility for the things we can control. We can interrupt the stress and on-going pressures that come along with crisis and limit the impact it can have on our bodies and minds. While the circumstances that we face may seem out of control, we can shift our focus by doing simple, routine activities that we do have control over.

God builds resilience in us as we simply obey Him. We follow the instructions in Romans 12:1, we "present our bodies as living sacrifices, holy and pleasing to God. This is your spiritual act of worship."

Taking care of yourself instills regularity in you and builds resilience. It allows health and well-being to support our doing good. It prepares you for the big hurdles that you may face.

In Psalm 18:1-2 the Lord reminds us of this strength: "I will love You, O Lord, my strength. The Lord is my rock and my fortress and my deliverer; my God, my strength, in whom I will trust; my shield and the horn of my salvation, my stronghold." (NKJV)

His strength in the unexpected

One way His strength showed up for me was on average, everyday dog walks. Our family ogled over our nine-and-a-half-pound Maltese Poodle mix named Lily. This dog. If I told you all the stories, you wouldn't believe them. You would have to see her ask for ice cream or minister love to a child to get the actual sense of her. She was my furry encourager and snuggled with me on any rough day, but walking was her love language. We would head out early because coastal North Carolina could whack you with humidity if you waited too late in the morning. So we did a loop that either went through a densely wooded park or followed the inside road around the subdivision. We set out at 7:15 a.m. with just enough time to make sure the kids were on their way.

This day was not unusual. Baggie shorts, old tennis shoes and my Duke University cap set the tone for our walk, pray and sweat session. For Lily, I brought enough water and a wide-topped water container to take two hydration breaks during our hour trek. When I had finished the radiation sessions that year, I committed to daily exercise, and I meant business. I planned on strengthening my immune system and muscles with these daily walks. But what I couldn't have planned was what else came with it.

We had walked two blocks when I took a different route and turned down a side street. After a few steps, I could hear music coming from a violin played by maybe a nine-year-old girl who looked to be waiting for the school bus. The closer I got to her, the sweeter the sound became. Was it the little ditty we sing to memorize our ABC's? No it was "Twinkle, Twinkle Little Star"! I knew it didn't matter. Each note she created produced a pure, light tone that resonated from the strings to anyone listening. The only audience was Lily and I. Lily wanted to stop and listen, so we did. The violinist was unaffected by our presence. She ended the song and carefully returned the instrument to its case.

I waved to her from across the street and said "Thank you! We really enjoyed your playing!" She smiled shyly.

We slowly walked on and then Lord said, "Come to me as a child." I knew the simplicity and humility He was pointing out. I responded, "Yes, Lord, I do want to have openness and vulnerability towards You." Then it dawned on me. He had nudged me on a different route from my routine path to show me something. He set up a scenario to soften my heart. It gave me strength because that act reminded me that He is always guiding me. It also encouraged me because I experienced Him in it.

We can plan ways to seek Him. In reaching out to Him, He promises us His strength. Then there are times when the Lord sets a stage to speak to us, reaching out to us. He seems to do this to show us His intentions, to make us aware of His presence, and to build strength in us.

He can give strength and security to the faintest heart in the most devastating hardship. He hears the cries of His own. He moves obstacles and makes a way where there seems to be no way. The strength He gives changes us as we go through difficulties. We receive that strength like a starving child receives nutrition from its mother. In the same way, what God gives us during that time of need, nurtures us. We mount up with wings like eagles. We run and don't faint. His strength restores us, making us resilient and able to go through impossible circumstances. Matthew 19:26 reminds us of Who we serve and depend on in these improbable and adverse situations. Repeat with me: "With men this is impossible; but with God all things are possible."

Surrender to receive strength

There are ways we can prepare our hearts to receive His strength. Whether we are going through a family crisis, a financial hardship, or as we wait on healing from a life-threatening disease, these principles can steady us. It doesn't always happen in a step-by-step order. But the process of allowing God's timing to become ours can be seen through these practices.

First, surrender your heart and your circumstances to God. If you look for ways to take over, put your foot down, or control the circumstances, the process will make you discouraged and distract you from the very closeness with God you need. He is patient and He will wait for you to let go. If you start with surrendering, your tender heart will be ready to receive from Him. This is the first step in processing emotions, fears, and grief in His Presence.

Second, strength comes from Him as we wait, so don't fight it. Go before Him and ask for a waiting posture. How can you seek and find encouragement and strength for your heart in the scriptures as you wait? He will point out the exact places to look. As the difficulty continues and seems to go on forever, embrace it anyway. Don't fight God's timing. God knows what should happen, when and why. He is working all things together for your good. God shoulders our suffering, walking with us through the onslaught, even as we experience it. He will cause you to grow and benefit from your waiting like nothing else you could do.

Third, stay connected to praying friends who offer wisdom, grace, and encouragement. There is no replacement for the friends and family who are there just when we need them most. They are ambassadors of God's love sent to your side to support your journey.

Our stories of suffering

This last point is the most important in dealing with people during your ongoing crisis. In growing resilience during our seasons of pain and suffering, please don't hide your vulnerability. In time, the Lord will make a way for you to share what you have gone through. He may bring someone who is going through something similar or has feelings about their hardships that you relate to. You hold the key to the door of hope that they need opened. Briefly give them the most honest telling of your experience that you can. Let them ask questions. Tell them about your pain, your doubts, and your discouragement. Help them to understand how you lost hope and how the Lord restored it. Pray with them to receive the Lord's strength. Encourage them to hold onto Him.

Everyone's details are different. I don't tell someone what to do if they are trying to decide what cancer treatments to receive, for instance. Their details are their own choices to pray through. Their case can be as different from mine as apples are from oranges. But what they do need from me is how I held on to the Lord, how I surrendered in prayer, and how the scriptures were my lifeline. They need to know how to keep relationships while they are navigating through their hard season. Show them the love of Jesus and your words and actions will be as good to them as grace and mercy.

We also share our suffering because we need the prayers of the righteous. James 5:16 reminds us: "The prayer of a righteous person is powerful and effective." The righteous, those in right standing with God, pray for others out of a heart that is rooted in the promises of God. If I believe that He is a rewarder of those who diligently seek Him, then I can pray for you and bring faith into your circumstance, no matter what it is.

Hebrews 11:6 reminds us that God "rewards those who earnestly seek Him." That seeking is what we often do on behalf of others who are simply too sick, weary, or beaten up by life to take the next step. We are there for each other in prayer because that is what Jesus demonstrates in His love for us. He continuously makes intercession on our behalf (Hebrews 7:25). Believers are connected to one another in a mysterious and glorious way. We make appeals to God who hears us and then moves in tandem with our prayers for His will to be done. When we are weak, we need others to pray for us. When we are well, we are the ones to lift those needing help. First Corinthians 12:26 says it best: "If one part suffers, all parts suffer with it, and if one part is honored, every part rejoices with it."

In his book, *How to Pray,* R.A. Torrey writes "The true purpose of prayer is that God may be glorified in the answer."[5] Does God receive glory as we come alongside another in their suffering and pray for His will to be done in their life? Yes. His body, the body of Christ, as we refer to believers, works organically to bear one another in prayer and in numerous other ways. Jesus said, "I tell you the truth, whatever you did for one of the least of these brothers and sisters of mine, you did for me." (Matthew 25:40)

Any time there is pain and suffering there is an opportunity to know the Lord in a way that you have never experienced before. Keep your focus fixed on Him through every peak and valley of this season. What He is doing for you is not only for your sake in bringing redemption, resolution to what you are going through, and growing resilient, He is also using your life to tell His story of love, hope and resurrection.

TAKEAWAYS

- Crisis fatigue is the term used to describe chronic stress and fatigue, which stems from prolonged crisis or adversity.
- Resilience is a major safeguard against the symptoms of crisis fatigue.
- Changing our mindset and actively working with what we can control in our lives can limit the effects of ongoing crises.
- When you are dealing with disease, you can practice nutritional and self-care routines that keep your body supported while it heals.
- God shoulders our suffering, walking with us through the onslaught, even as we experience it.

SPIRITUAL PRACTICE: SILENCE

Find a place where you can be uninterrupted. Spend some time just being quiet. Think of this time as sitting in silence *with* God. This may be a new experience. Focus your mind on His Presence being right there with you. Imagine yourself sitting by an open fire or on your deck at sunset with Him. Let His presence minister to your heart as you simply wait with Him.

When you are ready, ask God to bring to mind a particular situation you are facing. What does God want you to know? Then spend five more minutes in silent reflection, just listening to God. Respond to Him in prayer, stating the ways you will respond to His guidance today.

CHAPTER 5

Asking God Why

By inviting God into our difficulties, we ground life—even its sad moments—in joy and hope. When we stop grasping our lives, we can finally be given more than we could ever grab for ourselves. And we learn the way to a deeper love for others.

–Henri Nouwen[1]

AS HE DID EVERY MORNING, my son, Zachary, age three, had formed a cereal box semi-circle around his bowl. On the back of one of the boxes was a map of Christopher Columbus' route to the New World. He stared at the three ship replicas and drew his finger across the map printed on the box.

"Mom, when we take vacation can we visit Christopher Columbus?" His eyes were filled with wonder as he thought about meeting old Chris.

I picked him up from the breakfast table and sat him on the vanity in the bathroom to make eye contact with him.

"Zachary, Christopher Columbus lived a long, long time ago. He isn't alive anymore."

"CHRISTOPHER COLUMBUS IS DEAD?" he screamed. "DOES GOD KNOW WHAT HE DID?"

"Honey, remember when we went to grandpa's funeral?" The previous months had been ones of grief and simply letting go of my dad, the one who had provided wisdom throughout my life. My father's passing brought deep sorrow. But even now, his death was illustrating God's sovereignty to his grandson.

Zachary nodded. "I remember." He pouted sternly.

"Every person has a time to live on the earth and then God brings them home to heaven to live with Him there forever. Just like He did with your grandpa."

His cherub face fell into a sad frown. His bottom lip quivered slightly. "Even me?"

It was a lot for his young mind to take in. I tried to console him. I swept him up in a mama bear's hug and explained a difficult reality with simple truth. "You will have a long, long time to live your life before that happens."

Crocodile tears trickled down his cheeks "Mom," he choked out, "I just want to see it snow one more time."

"Oh honey! You will see it snow again!"

It touched my heart so deeply to see how anguished he was at the thought of dying. He forgot all about meeting Christopher Columbus as he considered death. His innocent questions showed me his heart, who he was as a person, and how he was forming his own beliefs even at this young age. His concerns gave me a snapshot of who he was and who he would become, a man of sincerity, sensitivity, and honesty.

If you are a parent, you can recall the years of your toddler endlessly asking "Why...". They are difficult because their answers are usually too large for a toddler to understand. That's if we can even come up with a plausible answer. Why does the sun hurt my eyes? Because it's an enormous ball of fire. Why do I have to hold your hand to cross the street? To keep you safe. But why do I need to be safe? Because you could get hit by a car if the driver doesn't see you. Or why do I need to eat broccoli? Because vegetables help us stay healthy. But why do we need to be healthy? Umm...

Why can't dogs talk? I don't know. I wish they could. The why questions are typically followed by another why question, reminders of our own desire for understanding. No matter our age, we long for understanding.

We rely on God to answer our questions. We want to understand life from His perspective. We want life's difficulties to have reasonable purposes attached to them. That longing is not any different when we are facing insurmountable pain and suffering. We lean on God for comfort and healing. Along with His love and guidance, along with the hope of better days, we ask God to explain why with hopes of gaining the purpose for our suffering. Asking God why opens our heart to Him. But even if I understand all the reasons why, I will still need to trust Him.

Our innocent queries reveal our hearts to God. They demonstrate our desires, our hopes and how our beliefs are being formed by our struggles. Our concerns show us who we are and where the tensions are located. They are snapshots of our most vulnerable selves.

A loving father

Just as Zachary knew he needed help from me understanding how long he could live, we know that our understanding comes from God. We come to Him in the middle of our crisis wanting to understand it. When we ask Him why, we look to Him for what we need to navigate through times of pain and suffering. By asking why, we hope that in understanding the big picture, it will help us trust His guidance in our smaller-sized need for answers. But in our seeking answers, will finding them help us to trust Him?

What could follow in His response may not be the answers we were hoping for at all. Zachary simply wanted a yes to his vacation plans. His shock turned to anguish when he realized Columbus was no longer on planet earth. He thought: wait, who is this God that allows the death of Christopher Columbus? We want to know why bad things are allowed by a loving and good Father. Just like a child, we can be shocked if God doesn't provide us with clear answers.

In the throes of pain and suffering, this question can present itself:

Is God the good Father that we have read about? Does He care when we are in seasons of pain and prolonged suffering? When suffering continues, we can begin to wonder if He has left us. Have we done something that caused the situation? When God doesn't provide us with answers, we might think that in our pain we have reached some mysterious limitation on His goodness. We can doubt our faith. Is it strong enough?

Knowing that our why's can open us to receiving from Him, we can honestly seek His perspective. The Bible assures us that we are welcome in God's presence as beloved children. "Let us then approach God's throne of grace with confidence, so that we may receive mercy and find grace to help us in our time of need."(Hebrews 4:16)

God refers to Himself as our heavenly Father. Our earthly fathers held us and comforted us, resting our small frames on their broad shoulders. Fathers wrestled with us as toddlers and tossed us into the air as we squealed. Fathers built trust and security into our lives through their loving direction and stability. God uses this relational term to explain how He relates to us. He created us to know and relate to Him as our formative, nurturing parent.

Jesus reveals God as the giver of all that is good, better than our earthly father. "If you, then, though you are evil know how to give good gifts to your children, how much more will your Father in heaven give good gifts to those who ask him!" he says in Matthew 7:11. He refers to his Father as "Our Father" as He taught His disciples how to pray: "'Our Father in heaven, hallowed be your name."(Matthew 6:9) Jesus calls us into a unified family. His heavenly Father is ours. We are to follow His lead in revering God when we pray. But far more, He is our Father. It is the origin of His connection to us. He created you to be in relationship with Him.

Tyler Staton, in *Praying Like Monks, Living Like Fools*, underscores our difficulty with praying to this loving Father. "We struggle to believe in a God as powerful, good, knowable, and loving as the one Jesus introduces us to. 'God is love.' (1 John 4:8) It's who he is, the summary of his character boiled down to a single, defining word. We buy that intellectually, but at a deeper level, somewhere in our emotions, in our bones, we don't trust it." It requires trust beyond our understanding to settle ourselves into the cocoon of God's love. When we say "our Father" in the Lord's Prayer, we are relying on the eternal and unending love expressed by His good nature. The remainder of our prayers rest on that belief. Staton continues by pointing to the significance of honoring God as we pray. We begin with His name, bowing to His infinite goodness. "It all starts and ends with remembering who we're talking to."[2]

In 1 John 3:1 we read: "See what love the Father has lavished on us, that we should be called children of God; and that is what we are." It is in that love we honor Him in our asking why, in our seeking to know Him, and perhaps in our acceptance of what we can and cannot understand. Nevertheless, we still must learn to trust Him. Pain and suffering do not erase His goodness or His heart toward us. Rather, adversity teaches us to trust who this heavenly Father is and just how deep His love is.

Another opportunity to trust

In 2012 I injured my ankle. After surgery I spent the better part of nine months in a lounge chair, reading, resting and making art. Once the ankle healed, I needed to relearn to walk.

I had not been out of that lounge chair long before my endocrinologist ordered an ultrasound, my safety net for catching recurrent thyroid cancer. Because of the failed nuclear thyroid treatment, I had to repeat ultrasound scans every six months. The Lord's kindness did not escape me. Looking back, I see that He allowed the timing of this scan *after* I was on my feet and fully healed from the surgery. And this scan brought bad news: my thyroid cancer had returned.

That same year (2012), my husband suffered a major heart attack just months after winning a national racquetball championship and climbing to the summit of a 14,000-foot mountain. I remember the discouragement of discovering that the cancer had returned, the exhaustion of being a caregiver to my husband, and the hope that the Lord infused us both with. Through God's grace, resilience had become a reflex. Within months after my surgery, I began teaching art.

Resilient faith is built as we recall the times the Lord made a way through a crisis, just as the Hebrews were taught to remember how God had parted the Red Sea for them to pass through. God provides when we are given strength in the moment, creating in us a determination that comes from nowhere. Even when we do not know how we got to the other side of our Red Sea, He provides and somehow, as we refuse to give up, we are on dry land.

Praying our questions

When we ask our listening and loving heavenly Father a question, we are invited into a dialogue with Him. He may point us to a verse, reveal His heart of understanding our concerns by comforting us, or let us soak in His presence. In asking God questions, we reveal our hearts and see our relationship with Him. Are we trusting completely? Our tone can show us what we need to submit to Him. Are we trying to escape or deny the reality of what's going on? We might hear it in the denial our words express. Is there grief or anxiety wrapped around our "why God?" By listening to our questions, we become more aware of what our hearts hold.

Every child of God who has wondered about the purpose of pain in their life, has asked "Why this? Why now? Why me?" It makes sense that seeking God would also involve asking questions. It provides a dialogue between us and the author of life. Our queries reveal our heart, our concerns, and even our lack of trust in the One who is listening. When we approach our heavenly Father as His child seeking wisdom and encouragement, we start with believing that He hears us.

Just like Zachary wanted answers, we ask our Father questions because we trust that He knows the answers. With a toddler's innocence, Zachary was relying on a bridge of trust with me. He just wanted to know if he'd be allowed to live to see it snow one more time. Poor kid! We also build a bridge of trust with God in asking our heartfelt questions.

As we honestly seek God's guidance in walking through times of pain and suffering, we create a canvas in our hearts for Him to illustrate His wisdom. Maybe He won't give us the answer we think we need. But instead, He might lead our conversation in another direction with His wisdom. Maybe He is demonstrating that wisdom over time through events, conversations, with music on the radio, or through seemingly random circumstances. All of these are provided to illuminate our understanding of His heart toward us. We honor our Father's love by coming to Him with our doubts and uncertainties. No topic is off-limits.

We want to know that He is concerned with us, that he sees our struggles. Does the overwhelmed, grieving widow have a loving God who is hearing and guiding her? Does the patient who is waiting for the word "remission" have an omniscient God who is guiding his journey? Can you, as you face that heartbreak that separates you from fulfilling your dreams, ask God in that pain? Can you continue to hope and trust despite facing the unknown? Are you open to how He might answer? Then go ahead, ask. He fully gets us and knows we need to ask. But we act on what we believe of His nature because He always gives us the truth.

Just as a child asks why about everything from bugs to sidewalk boundaries, we form core beliefs by asking God questions. How God provides healing in the dialogue is a mystery and a wonder. But He does just that.

God has a plan

God is the author and creator of all and uses all things at His discretion. He orchestrates circumstances to move at His beck and call. He puts people into your path and mine to offer answers where we would least think to look. His wisdom springs from a loving, kind Father who is more than willing to build connections with us precisely when we need it most.

Look at the questions people asked God throughout scripture. Job was called "blameless and upright" (Job 1:8) by God and David was "a man after His own heart" (1 Samuel 13:14). They both asked Him why they were suffering and felt as though He had abandoned them. Jesus was His "beloved son with whom He was well pleased" (Matthew 3:17). In His suffering Jesus asked Him, "My God, my God, why have you forsaken me?" (Matthew 27:46) God did not always answer by solving their problems. He did offer them Himself. He showed them that He was with them, and His sovereignty was securely holding them.

God is in control of our lives no matter the circumstances or how dismal and dark it may seem. He will demonstrate His way for you to move through it all. He has a plan for you and for people in your life. He will never leave you or forsake you. That promise is guaranteed with the blood of Jesus.

As we know, our plan and God's plan may be very different. We don't get a road map and a timeline to follow. But we do get guidance and truth. When God's plan for us isn't what we want, we know that following Him will be for our best. If we are demanding, in foot-stomping fury, we have part of our answer as we demonstrate where we are. Our attitude is reflected in that fury. In our asking why are we asking to see if His reasons are something we would agree with? God assures us that understanding is not necessary. What He does require is obedience. In 1 Samuel 15:22 it tells us what is most important to God; "to obey is better than sacrifice."

I can honor Him when I don't understand His ways. That means I am accepting and flexible. I bend my ways to accept His ways because I trust His nature and goodness. That bending does not diminish my capabilities; it surrenders them to His will. I let go of my plans, my reasoning and my self-reliance. He is faithful. He cannot be any other way. He is always only good.

Moving from why to how

God always, without question, has a plan for our lives. But His plan may not be apparent. It may not even be on our radar. In moving our hearts toward acceptance, we begin to let go of demanding answers.

Instead, we can simply ask, "how can I align myself with You, God?" There it is again, surrender. Your surrender brings great peace with it.

As the Apostle Paul wrote, "Do not be anxious about anything, but in every situation, by prayer and petition, with thanksgiving, present your requests to God. And the peace of God, which transcends all understanding, will guard your hearts and your minds in Christ Jesus." (Philippians 4:6-7)

The early days of cancer made me wonder how God would provide. Would He supernaturally pour out peace when there only seemed to be anxiety at every turn? Would He make His way clear by giving me a road map through scripture to trust Him day by day? Would I learn to know Him better because of my weaknesses? Would He bring a Pool of Bethesda experience, and I wouldn't need the harsh treatments that doctors prescribed? During the Stage IV radiation summer, I was surrounded every day by women who were experiencing worse symptoms, negative outcomes, and focusing their attention on end-of-life preparations. Though I knew that God touches each of us individually, I couldn't explain the impact that their peacefulness had on me.

Nancy and I met in the radiation waiting area. There were usually four patients besides us. We knew them only from our weekly radiation appointments. Even though she had had a brain tumor removed weeks before, she came ready to chat, share, and pray. But this woman's joy did not match her diagnosis. She and her daughter wore a different colorful and whimsical-styled hat every time we met. They looked like they were headed to a birthday celebration instead of providing coverage for her surgical scars. Nancy and I became fast friends. Her jokes were as good as her prayers. The people providing me rides to radiation fought over who would take me next just so they could be part of what was taking place there. Before we got called back for radiation, we shared about the ways we saw the Lord's goodness in our lives. People in the waiting room absorbed every word because there was tangible hope wrapped around every conversation. I know God moved many caregivers' and family members' hearts to salvation because of those intimate discussions.

When Nancy went into hospice, she and I shared Psalm 103: 1-2 days before she entered eternity. We quoted it together from memory: "Bless the Lord, O my soul, and all this is within me, bless His holy name! Bless the Lord, O my soul, and forget not all His benefits..." (ESV) She softly described each person and moment that meant the most to her. "I am so grateful for the life He has given me. For my daughter especially, her children and their loving me so well. I am so glad I know Jesus and His love." She went on for several minutes. She held my hand tightly and wanted me to listen to every incidence of gratitude she spoke. She did not shed a tear, but I couldn't stop mine.

The dramatic and holy opportunity to walk closely with women like Nancy did not create panic or doubt. They offered me just the opposite. I saw how faith made death less fearful and more of a spiritual transition, His hand holding ours as we walk together into eternity. I saw each woman do just that and trust Him with their transition into glory. I knew that if the Lord called me home and eternity waited for me, I had seen Him hold others and lead them through. I knew He would surely do the same for me.

God's plan for us begins as we acknowledge His will for our lives beyond what we plan or can make sense of. When suffering threatens, He reminds us that He has our lives securely held in His righteous, right hand. "Be not dismayed, for I am your God; I will strengthen you, I will help you, I will uphold you with my righteous right hand." (Isaiah 41:10) When we open ourselves to accept His will, it strengthens the bridge of trust between us.

The benefits of processing emotions

God brings healing and wholeness from my pain if I allow him access to my heart. He is the engineer of my life's journey, but I am the doorkeeper of my feelings, attitudes and issues. As I process my pain in His presence, He reveals his goodness. As I confess, see my weaknesses, be alright with my story, and accept myself before Him, I build inner strength and a resilient faith.

I process my pain in His presence, because I have come to know the benefits. He reveals his goodness and develops wholeness in the bonds of relationship. I allow my heart to receive His strength and over time the suffering and pain becomes something else. The pain receives His goodness; His grace and I become more whole. Opening up to Him during painful seasons is opening up to the Potter's careful and tender hands. "Like clay in the hand of the potter, so are you in my hand..." (Jeremiah 18:6). He has used the pain of life to transform my heart.

When you gain an ability to process and express emotions, especially those that are difficult or uncomfortable, you strengthen your ability to see yourself. Processing before the Lord allows self-awareness to open gateways to receiving His grace, forgiveness, and hope. If I am okay with who I am, I am not operating from shame. My eyes are more open to others' needs. Processing before the Lord allows empathy to grow and improves self-acceptance.

Some ways to become more emotionally vulnerable to the Lord include:

- Keep a journal. Record your thoughts and feelings. This is not a diary of things you've done, but a documentation of where you are traveling spiritually.
- Become more honest with God and others about your earnest needs. Pray for a knowledge of the difference between your wants and needs.
- Name your feelings, become more aware of what you feel and why. Share that with God and see how He responds.
- Spend one hour per week discussing emotionally difficult things out loud and with another person.
- Allow anger before the Lord and deal with it with Him.
- Be clear about what you want to eat, what entertainment you want to watch with your spouse or friends. Practice clarity and honesty as you communicate.

After using journal writing to process her deep-seated grief, Sheryl Sandberg began to notice the benefits it brought. "Journaling can help you make sense of the past as you rebuild your future." She quotes philosopher Soren Kierkegaard, "life can only be understood backward but it must be lived forward."[3] We use strategies of resilience to access strength while we process our emotions. Journaling supports that process and creates a pathway to move forward while navigating difficulties.

The comfort in vulnerability

Vulnerability comes from the Latin word for "wound." It is the state of being open to injury or attack. Emotional vulnerability is something different. It creates a powerful openness to God and to others that says, "here I am, scars, wounds and all." It comes with emotional exposure that brings a degree of uncertainty. It involves learning how to be willing to accept the emotional risk that comes from being open and willing to love and be loved.

Brené Brown, author and researcher, says: "Giving feedback, receiving feedback, problem-solving, ethical decision-making... These are all born of vulnerability."[4] Our curious minds can develop wisdom, discover, learn and express creativity. All of these skills take time to develop, and they require courage to build.

Our struggles, hardships, and crises can bring long seasons of discomfort. It is in these long periods of discomfort *before* the problems are resolved that resilience is growing.

Resilience is cultivated best when we don't know where we're headed, when changes around us multiply, as we goof-up, make mistakes and adjust to the difficulties surrounding us. Our struggles, hardships, and crises can bring long seasons of discomfort. It is in these long periods of discomfort *before* the problems are resolved that resilience is growing. Getting feedback and problem-solving while we are seeking solutions are the inner workings of forming vulnerability and resilience.

The line in a Beatles' song suggests that the long and winding road leads us home.[5] Resilience grows best the more comfortable we are with being uncomfortable while traveling that long and winding road. If we tolerate our uncertainty before our problems are corrected, we are teaching ourselves to be flexible, to bend, to breathe, while things are disrupted.

Vulnerability allows us the courage to seek and find, to test and attempt possibilities. The seeds of vulnerability support and nurture the growth of resilience. If we are okay to not be okay, as we hold on to God and seek and find answers, personal growth will happen. When the trial and error of problem-solving continues, and we endure, resilience grows. It's on the road of hardship and difficulties as we ask and give feedback that resilience is cultivated. This long and winding road, as a matter of fact, does lead us home. To Him.

James 1:4-5 (AMP) underscores the process: "And let endurance have its perfect result and do a thorough work, so that you may be perfect and completely developed [in your faith], lacking in nothing. If any of you lacks wisdom [to guide him through a decision or circumstance], he is to ask of our benevolent God."

If we can apply Brown's emphasis on asking questions to our relationship with God, we can begin to see the value God places in processing our emotions before Him.

In the give and take of being open with Him we understand how important our questions are. He uses them as pieces on a chess board. We ask and He will move a verse, a person, a circumstance on the board of our lives in answering us. We notice the condition of our hearts. While in pain and suffering, can I ask God hard questions without dishonoring Him? Can I ask because I know He is willing to answer? Can I follow Him in the work of giving and receiving feedback from Him? Can I trust that He knows and accepts me as I approach His throne of grace? Can I believe my spiritual ears as I actually hear Him respond to me with vivid and stark truth?

Forming a vulnerable relationship with God means moving, bending, and flexing at His lead. We stay connected with Him because we have required ourselves to be as honest with Him about where we are;

as honest and open as we can possibly be. If there is anger, be angry but don't act on it. If there is grief, grieve with Him in the hope we have been promised. Any and every emotion is offered a safe place for expression before our loving Father.

Seeing His plan and purpose

The Bible story of Joseph and his brothers illustrates how God uses bad circumstances for good. Joseph's brothers captured and sold him into slavery. He ended up in prison where things deteriorated. Nevertheless, God brought him to a place of authority in the Egyptian palace. God proved that He had a plan all along. Joseph's reign could not have been timed any better for his brothers. They were in Judea starving because of a drought. God uses Joseph's authority to provide them food during a famine. In Genesis 50:20 Joseph speaks to his brothers, "You intended to harm me, but God intended it for good to accomplish what is now being done, the saving of many lives."

Could this be how God is planning to use difficulty in our lives? Could He be using the difficulty and crisis for our good? Could the circumstance of what appears to be evil be used by God to grow stronger faith? Does God intend to use the hardships to grow resilience in your life? The thing that seems like opposition could be the very resistance that God is using to make your faith stronger, to grow your dependence on Him, to nurture your relationship with Him. This is all part of His good plan for your good. As Ephesians 1:11 states: "In Him we were also chosen, having been predestined according to the plan of Him who works out everything in conformity with the purpose of His will."

We all have misunderstandings and interpretations of what God's will is for our lives. It is part of being human to exercise our will. He tells us we are given a different life than the one we had before. But each of us must learn what that means.

It took some doing for me to acknowledge His sovereignty and authority over the plans and desires I had for my life. Initially I thought that God was signing onto my plan when I first committed my life to Him. What I didn't expect was the tearing down of my will and jettisoning of my ways that needed to take place. I had to learn through difficult experiences to deny myself. In that act of surrender, done again and again, I learned to replace my will with His. I had to let go of my "grasping life" as Nouwen describes it. Then I could receive His life in me. I earnestly believed He would accomplish Kingdom purposes as I simply obeyed. And He did. But what I didn't expect was the need to bring all aspects of myself into submission.

2 Corinthians 10:5 does not overstate the process. "We demolish arguments and every pretension that sets itself up against the knowledge of God, and we take every thought to make it obedient to Christ." The Amplified Version describes those issues as "every proud and lofty thing that sets itself up against the [true] knowledge of God."

Sometimes those are the very things that keep us from knowledge of God. They are not arguments, but vain, proud, and lofty imaginations we hold about ourselves.

When I let go of what I wanted for my life, I could receive His life in me. Galatians 2:20 puts it into proper perspective. "I have been crucified with Christ; and it is no longer I that live, but Christ that lives in me: and the life which I now live in the flesh I live in faith." We all have misunderstandings about what His life in us means. What exactly do I let go of? Answer: all of it.

As we pray in the Lord's Prayer (found in Matthew 6:9-13), we are asking Him for what He intends to do through our lives. "Your kingdom of love come on earth, in my life, as it is in heaven." But we know that what we are praying for is not wrapped in glitter with a decorative bow. It took some doing for me to acknowledge His sovereignty and authority over my plans and desires. What about your surrender? Did you offer your whole life understanding that is what God's plan requires?

We are being given a way in Him to perceive and receive His goodness. But our lives in God's Kingdom were never intended to be easy or comfortable. "Take up your cross and follow Me." He specifies this act. You must deny yourself in order to take hold of His life for you. (Matthew 16:24) This is not how anyone would start a public relations campaign. We are not drawn to sacrifice itself. We are drawn by His love and our need for it.

Seeing His goodness and being His goodness in our messy situations comes as we surrender to His will. It takes sacrifice. Exchanging my will for His abolishes our control. His good plan for a renewed life is not our plan plus His power. We are not promised ease, a comfortable life. We are living out His plan, on the earth, in our lifetime, by walking with Him daily. Why? So that we can become more like Jesus.

Seeing His goodness and being His goodness in our messy situations comes as we surrender to His will. It takes sacrifice.

It is part of being human to exercise our will instinctively. It is the act of new life being born in us through Jesus' death that calls us to lay it all down. He tells us we are given a different life than the one we had before. We learn what that means by dying to self, experiencing pain and suffering, and holding onto Him as He resurrects His Spirit in us.

When we pray in the Lord's Prayer, "Your kingdom come; your will be done, on earth," in my life, "as it is in heaven," (Matthew 6:10), we are asking Him for what He intends to do through our lives. He intends to establish His Kingdom in us.

You have a better life because of His leadership, His being God and because He knows the end of all things. It is a better life because He walks with us in it. It can seem that it is filled with pain and suffering at times. But in all of this, He is bringing His kingdom and Himself to us and through us.

While living through difficult circumstances, He is working His plan into us. His good plan is that we are changed into the image and likeness of Jesus. As Romans 8:29 promises, "...those God foreknew He also predestined to be conformed to the image of His Son."

Not stuck in our suffering

When hardships continue, when deep and prolonged grief faces us, or when suffering is pronounced and extreme, our faith is tested. We can feel our circumstances are trapping us in anger, isolation, or self-absorption, unable to find the way through it.

God has provided the community of believers for comfort, encouragement, practical support and accountability. When we are stuck in suffering, we need others. When we are lonely and fighting battles that we shouldn't fight alone, we need to reach out--even though it's not easy to ask for prayer. As we bear another's burdens in prayer, provide mutual encouragement and celebrate each other's victories, we build connection. When others triumph, I celebrate with them. When they grieve, we grieve together. Our faith grows when we choose to let faithful friends know the pain we are experiencing. God's comfort is meant to be shared. "We are confident that as you share in our sufferings, you will also share in the comfort God gives us." (2 Corinthians 1:7, NLT)

Recently a long-time friend had no choice but to walk through a divorce. She sought God's wisdom about this heartbreaking decision. As she struggled to seek help and find godly counsel, she experienced several critical health problems one after the other. She had to quickly make medical decisions. She needed rest when she recovered from surgeries and support when she was discouraged. All the while she needed to be reminded that the Lord was carrying her through the battle. As the months passed, I encouraged her with prayer, timely verses, and art to remind her of God's beauty. Sometimes homemade chicken soup was just what the doctor ordered.

Before she was sick, this friend had regularly gathered newcomers to our church with other women to spark conversations and relationships. She had been the one to initiate birthday celebrations and lunches in our prayer group. As she became too sick to follow through, others in our group handled the details that ended up helping her. What she had accomplished in providing a connection for others through setting up meetings and text threads had become a way for us to minister to her. When she had prayer requests, they were disseminated through the network she had created. The natural result of her gift of hospitality to others then became the means of supporting her. "Give and it will be given to you. ...For with the measure you use, it will be measured to you." (Luke 6:38)

God builds resilience as we support each other through the difficulties. He provides a community, building not made with human hands. It is the body of Christ, everyday saints who demonstrate His love in active, practical ways. Ephesians 3:17-18 underscores this message: "... I pray that you, being rooted and established in love, may have power, together with all the Lord's holy people, to grasp how wide and long and high and deep is the love of Christ..." The "you" Paul writes to in his letters in the New Testament is plural: the community of believers.

"If you want to go fast, go alone. But if you want to go far, go together." The origins of this saying go back to East, West and South Africa where tribal communities were dependent on endurance and traveling wide stretches of Sahara to hunt for food. Their lives depended on each one in the community playing a crucial role in their survival. Together they could go far. Today we can't always see that our spiritual stamina rests on the shoulders of our fellow-believers. Want to go far, to endure and go the distance with the Lord? Then we do that best together.

Resilience formed in suffering

God is the lover of our souls and provides ways through our struggles with pain. Tim Keller, in *Walking with God through Pain and Suffering* points out what times of pain can provide. "One of the main ways we move from abstract knowledge about God to a personal encounter with Him as a living reality is through the furnace of affliction. Believers understand many doctrinal truths in the mind, but those truths seldom make the journey down into the heart except through disappointment, failure, and loss."[6] In this journey we confront what we truly believe about God's character. Is He good? Is He faithful? Will He ever leave me in my suffering? Suffering requires us to dig deep and face our doubts. It magnifies our weaknesses, that otherwise, we can tend to forget.

God's love, His plan, and His goodness are the reasons we become more resilient while facing pain and suffering. No matter the circumstances, He provides Himself. He is the one who gives us the strength to persevere when we suffer. In Romans 8:35 we are told of the absolute security of His love. "Who shall separate us from the love of Christ? Shall trouble or hardship or persecution or famine or nakedness or danger or sword?"

My miracle is a testimony of His faithfulness. Because I lived, I get to see grandchildren grow. I get to see it snow one more time. Each day I live I am offered life's simple daily miracles, even in the difficulties. The struggles, the hardships, the crises that come offer me an opportunity to build resilient faith in the One who is holding onto me even as I suffer. As I persevere in the suffering, resilient faith is growing. It is an invisible process. I can't see it being formed, but I can build it with my faithfulness to Him.

TAKEAWAYS

- Asking God questions in humility opens up our heart to Him for His responses.
- We ask God why with hopes of understanding the purpose of our suffering.
- Asking God questions creates a canvas in our hearts for Him to illustrate His wisdom.
- We can worship God while having questions and doubts, creating a space in our hearts for honoring Him.
- Surrendering my will for His is a life-long process that is meant to abolish our control.

SPIRITUAL PRACTICE: VULNERABILITY

Offer yourself acceptance and self-compassion in an effort to develop vulnerability with friends, at work or school, and with God. Be open to sharing thoughts and feelings with people you trust. Seek ways the Lord may provide to build sincerity and openness.

In communicating your needs, in allowing others into your thoughts, desires, and fears, are you building a stronger sense of who you are? In becoming more aware of how you listen, give your full attention to others' viewpoints and attempt to understand where they are coming from.

Pay attention to the ways you have become more vulnerable when sharing with friends. How does an awareness of this process affect your vulnerability before God?

CHAPTER 6
Reframing for Redemption

Troubles are often the tools by which God fashions us for better things.

–Henry Ward Beecher[1]

IT WAS A TYPICAL BRUSHFIRE. Temperatures had rested in the triple digits for weeks. The humidity, nonexistent. With no rain for months, the trees and ground cover were waiting fuel for any spark. When the underbrush catches it can quickly escalate into a raging wildfire. They happen frequently this time of year. The forests to our west are national forests so Cal Fire, the National Park Service, and U.S. Forest Services responded to this one. Their combined efforts would bring it under control.

When thick smoke rose over the western mountains that day, the local news told us not to panic; no one in our valley or in the surrounding areas was in danger. Don't worry, said the news. Remain calm.

That night, like any other July night, residents of our city of 92,000 went to bed thinking about normal summer issues: skyrocketing temperatures and where to go on vacation. No one was on alert. It was just another sweltering evening in the valley.

What the morning sun revealed was shocking. Our western sky was lit up in flames like the lighting on a western movie set. Backlight in an orange-reddish glow, the outline of the hills warned of approaching disaster. "Remain calm," the local newscaster said. "The firefighters have it under control. We are monitoring the situation very closely and will alert you of any changes." But we didn't need to watch the television to see the progress of the fire. Everyone looked west to see what the fire was doing. Hour by hour it steadily made its way to Redding. Staying calm was the last thing that felt right.

Redding's city limits are bordered on three sides by mountains, the Trinity Mountains to the west, Mt. Shasta to the north and Lassens to the east. Homes and ranches are scattered off rural backroads. The fire encroached the outlying areas and was steadily gaining ground as it burned barns and outbuildings in the western hills and then threatened the small, historic town of Lake Shasta. People in those areas were told to evacuate. Just as a precaution.

The local news gave hourly updates to an anxious audience. The fire that had started less than 24 hours ago was now a full-fledged wildfire, headed straight for us. Smoke filled the valley, and an eerie-orange film shrouded the sun. By afternoon, the fire moved from forested underbrush to the roofs of houses in the outlying subdivisions. Soon Interstate 5 south was blocked with cars clogging the off-ramps and inching along, with nowhere to go.

We were assured that the Sacramento River would be a barricade protecting the remainder of the town. It's a natural fire break, they explained. No fire could jump the width of the river. As a precaution though, our friends from the west side joined us and soon we were housing three extra families, their children, grandchildren, and dogs. We packed go-bags with essentials and waited from our safe location on the east side, pinned to the television. Two RVs were packed beside our house, ready in case we needed a home on wheels.

From our business, which is located on the west side, we could see the flames that shot up higher than the foothills. The Convention Center, to our immediate north, appeared less than its two stories in comparison to the height of those flames. Horses and livestock that had sought safety at the rodeo arena and stables just past the Convention Center were now having to be moved again. Hour by hour the fire's status continuously changed as it tracked closer and closer to us.

The latest news report promoted the Fire Chief's assurance, "The river will protect us from the fire moving into town."

Wildfire!

At first it seemed that the fire's perimeters were being contained. News reports showed firefighters creating fire breaks by bulldozing the vegetation. Planes thundered overhead like scenes from a war zone. Orange streaks of fire retardant were steadily released to prevent the blaze from gaining ground.

People gathered in the Safeway parking lot, looking to the west, trying to see just how close it was to them. On the third night the fire had taken 7,000 acres. Keeping the fire out of the city was no longer possible.

That night a phenomenon called a fire tornado, something many didn't know existed, jumped the Sacramento River, and shot straight up a canyon burning homes and exploding trees that stood in its path. Civilians and firefighters were killed. The Carr fire became the sixth largest fire in California history. It was an event that would change the way we looked at wildfires and our safety while living in a fire-prone, yet beautiful valley.

This event changed how we look at tragedy and trauma in our area. No longer could we think that the unthinkable would not happen. Now we are preparing for the unthinkable that could happen in our area again. Because of the escalation and the fire tornado, we experienced a paradigm shift.

We know our susceptibility to danger as humans on our ever-changing earth, but how we think about disasters has changed. Now, rather than wondering if they will happen, we will be thinking about how to survive them when they do happen.

The Carr fire destroyed 229,651 acres. At least 1,077 homes were destroyed, and hundreds damaged. But the starkest statistic was the loss of life. Three firefighters and five civilians were killed. Two of those were children. But as we know in any natural disaster, the statistics describe the impact, but don't tell the whole story. The story of how someone survived an event defines what was lost and what is gained from surviving such a disastrous event. The following is such a story.

A survivor's story

Dr. Carter, a dentist who lived in Redding, was frantic. She knew the smoke was filling the neighborhood and the fire was getting closer. When she saw her neighbor's houses were in immediate danger and the flames were coming closer, she knew it was time to go. She and her husband could only get a block closer to their gated entrance when the flames reached their car. There was nowhere to go. The only choice was to run for it.

"My husband told me 'If you want to live you have to run!' So, I ran as fast as I could, as a wall of fire came closer. I'm seeing deer, fawns, rats, and rabbits are all running. And I say to myself, they must know the way. So, I ran with them. I lost track of my husband but kept running. I ran to the bottom of the hill when I saw two policemen directing traffic. I had no idea where I was. The policeman said I had run four miles."

When Dr. Carter and her husband, Dr. Fard, later told their story to a reporter, she said, "I wish I would have known even one hour or even 20 minutes would have helped. But now everything is gone. It was so calm right before we saw the fire coming. I have lost my history, all my pictures and memories." Then her husband added, "But we are celebrating what we have. We gained a new life."[2]

The incredible story of running from a fire demonstrates this woman and man's intense desire to survive. They made quick decisions and took risks. They ran barefoot down a three-mile stretch of forested hills. They lived to tell the story about how they are moving forward.

As we hear their story of running for their lives, we are with them.

It's almost as if we are running down the hill as fast as we can. We live through her words. We feel her desire to survive and outrun the fire, as if we experienced it ourselves. As we listen, we experience that will to survive that is in all of us. Will they make it out of the fire's raging path? Will we make it out of our disasters? We believe that they will make it as we listen. We follow their story, believing that we will make it out to tell ours.

Dr. Carter set up survivor's boxes for those in need in the weeks immediately following their escape. Those boxes included provisions for those made homeless by the fire. She has been impacted by the loss, but she was also keenly aware of her strength. She understood the sense of loss and their gratitude for having survived. She chose to give to those impacted and hurting. She also chose to give hope by telling her story.

Making sense of it all

Adversity does not discriminate. Every person experiences some level of it, regardless of life circumstances. It is a caustic, harrowing, and character-forming reality. The emphasis is not on whether a hardship will happen, it is when it does happen, what will be our response? Will we have the faith, strength, or endurance to face it and bounce back? Will we, even in our pain, use the resources that God provides us? Will we be able to move forward despite the pain that a crisis can produce? Will we come back from it resilient? Will we bend from the impact but retain a resilient faith? Will we survive?

We may have experienced a betrayal that couldn't be resolved, the loss of a parent, a dissolved dream job, or an unfortunate financial hardship. Perhaps a natural disaster struck without warning, bringing severe repercussions. Experiencing a tornado, a hurricane, a week-long snowstorm, or a destructive earthquake, can shake us. When these events impact our sense of security, stability or livelihood, our perspective about the future is affected. But trials like these provide an opportunity to build resilience, even as we navigate through the trauma.

We can ask God how to recover from such disasters. We can lean into Him to make sense of it all. We can grow from the hardships given time, which can bring with it needed perspective. Without understanding why, we can formulate truth after adversity: truth about ourselves, our inner strength, and about how God is with us, helping us to heal.

Getting past the past

In Vivian Gornick's book, *The Situation and the Story*, she explores how voice shapes a story. She draws a distinction between an event or situation, and our story about that same event. Two people might see the same event differently. An individual might see it differently at different times.[3]

When I read Gornick's book, I was in the middle of creating an art curriculum for high school girls. Each art project began with questions they'd respond to in journals. They created images to translate their thoughts and feelings into pictures or symbolic images.

For this project I began by using Gornick's principle and coupled her thoughts with what I knew the Lord used to bring emotional healing from trauma. I could see how events that sometimes reroute our lives happen not because of the details, though harrowing, but because in our mind, we don't allow them to nurture or change us for the better.

When we access a traumatic memory of an event, the doom and anxiety of that issue plays repeatedly in our mind. Instead of becoming teachers for our good, the recalled disaster can stunt our development. However, if we can replace the takeaway from the event with a phrase that brings hope and maybe even gratitude, the message we repeat to ourselves is productive and promotes healing.

When it was time to launch this project, I began the session by explaining a disastrous circumstance that happened to me.

When I was a freshman in college, I carefully drove my brand-new red Volkswagen to visit my uncle. On the way back to school, I stopped at an intersection in response to a red blinking light, and the car to my left stopped too. I predicted she was waiting on me, but as I entered the intersection, so did she.

Her car hit my left bumper leaving a dent a third of the VW's size. My bottom lip hit the steering wheel as my head whiplashed from the impact. Six stitches later, I was given my first ticket with an invitation to traffic court. The charge: failure to stop at a blinking red light.

This event rattled me. I felt doomed. The shock of the accident, the unfair citation, and the newness of college weighed on me. I felt that even if I tried something new, bad would come of it. Though I didn't know it, I was experiencing a trauma symptom. I had the sense of the inevitable next shoe dropping.

After I described my event to the class of twelve fourteen- to sixteen-year-old students, I used the white board to separate my accident into stages: the before, during and after categories. I talked about the amount of time it took me to put the accident into a less traumatic perspective. As a result, I could override the doom I initially felt.

It only took a moment of thought before one student began telling her story. "The day my dad left I was so mad," the young girl wearing a pink, peace sign graphic tee, solemnly recounted. "I was so hurt and so confused, I couldn't talk to anyone for days. Even though both my mom and dad said things wouldn't change, I knew they were just saying that because they felt they had to." She looked down at her feet. A few of the other students shuffled in their seats nervously.

"I love my parents, but why couldn't they get their lives together and just work it out? My brother and I were scared for a long time."

I thanked her for her honesty and pointed the class toward the goal: "We are looking at these events as they took place in our past. Soon we will reframe them to lessen their negative impact." I directed a hopeful mantra to the student in the pink tee shirt: "Your story is about to get a better ending."

Another hand went up. "When my grandmother died last November, I thought I wouldn't have anywhere to live. For about a year she had taken care of me when my mom was sick. My grandma and I were so close. She taught me how to sew, and we spent rainy days cutting out patterns and sewing clothes for the school year." Her voice became softer. "I can't change any of it…"

"I am so sorry for your loss!" I said. "No, we can't change the facts. But we can change the way we use those facts. We can reframe our reaction to them." She nodded, agreeing.

The next girl to speak was older and had not shared much throughout the year. She wore heavy eyeliner, had unkempt, long black hair and baggy jeans. She looked at no one and explained what it felt like when she entered foster care. "I mean, foster care was rough. No one took the time to really care. The first and second homes creeped me out. I couldn't stay there. Then I got placed with a real family. I don't know why they were different. But for me, I felt like I belonged. I meant something to them."

At their young ages they had plenty of stories to tell. The girls all sat wide-eyed as I walked to the whiteboard and wrote the words "before, during, and after" across the top of the board.

"Now you will dissect the parts of your stories," I explained. "You are going to condense your stories into these three segments. In your journals, write the facts of what it was like before, during, and then after your event."

When they were finished, I began to discuss the beauty of living through an adverse situation. I suggested ways we can control how we think about circumstances that happen to us after we've had time to gain some perspective about it. Our brains help us to recover. They store our thoughts, feelings, and words about the event. Even months afterwards we may be looping that old tape with negative messages.

When we reframe that information, we can replay it again and again with healthy information. It becomes the new tape we play when we access memories about what happened and how it impacted us.

I was shocked to hear their takeaway statements after the exercise. They wanted to become the directors of their narrative. They were able to make statements perceiving their situation from different vantage points. Time had given them space to see things differently. They were able to say helpful and hopeful things in summarizing how they wanted to continue thinking about that adverse event.

The young girl who watched her father leave said, "it hurt when he left, but his leaving helped relieve tension in our home. There was less anger. After a while his leaving helped us to get along."

The student who was still grieving the death of her grandmother put a new frame around her dying. "I am using my grandmother's sewing machine to help me remember our times together. I'm thinking about making a pillow using her favorite colors for my bed."

The student who had a season in foster care joined in with her reframed perspective. "Because of this new family in foster care, I began to see how families work. After I rejoined my real family, I could see how my bad choices had affected my parents and siblings. It helped us get along."

Applying the reframing process

The same principle of reframing works for all of us. Initially, we describe the event and how it happened: who, what, when, and where. For example, a car accident would be explained by telling which car did what action and what happened in sequential steps. But whoever explains that situation and where they are when it took place makes all the difference.

Each person's description about that car accident would vary by how close they were to the accident and what they experienced. If they were in the car, their first-hand experience would be told differently than someone observing it from the sidewalk. There is a great deal of difference between what happened in a particular situation, and the story we tell ourselves about it afterwards.

Your memories about a traumatic event can keep you from growing and learning from your experience. The event may have impacted your emotions causing fear, anger, and mistrust to cloud your thinking at the time. Negative thoughts associated with the trauma could have shaped how you framed the situation then.

What I want to offer you is a way to look at this event and arrive at a redemptive truth. By reframing that event you can receive God's grace and healing as you process it with a newly formed perspective.

You can see it with new eyes. You are the director of your story. You can choose the validity of feelings, thoughts, and meaning you have had about the situation. You cannot change what happened, but you can change how it affects you moving forward.

The Lord orchestrates circumstances to draw our attention. He focuses our heart to long for release and renewal from Him. In Isaiah 44:22 it speaks about the redemption coming through Jesus. "I have swept away your offenses like a cloud, your sins like the morning mist. Return to me, for I have redeemed you."

Kasey Van Norman, therapist and author of *Nothing Wasted*, describes this process this way: "Our story is God's raw material for the new things He is building. This is why our past, not to be dismissed, downplayed, or undefined but instead is to be used as the resource to rebuild and restore us."[4]

Redemption in reframing a past event is when His mercy and grace reach into our hearts, and He guides us into healing. He redeems the situation not by changing it, but by changing our minds about it. He walks with us into the past event because He knows some aspect of it needs restoration. In order to receive His guidance, we must be open to Him and surrender to His timing and purpose. He offers empowerment by giving us freedom from its bondage.

Perhaps I have lingering pain from the event or from the people that were involved. Perhaps I see myself as the victim and I need to detach from that identity. Or maybe I haven't experienced forgiveness and am still bound by the weight of regret. No matter what holds me back, reframing my story after an adverse situation is a pathway toward redemption.

The diagnosis of Stage IV breast cancer froze me in my tracks. Fear, anxiety and then fatigue stifled my ability to think about choices concerning treatment options. Because I expected the Lord to provide me with a verse to focus on as He had with the first cancer episode, I was shaken when that didn't happen. My fear brought doubt that shook my sense of security. But that downward emotional spiral was stopped when the Lord drew my attention to the past cancer episode when I had managed fear with His steady support.

Redemption came as I sensed His peace and focused on the phrase "His faithfulness is new every morning" (Lamentations 3:23). I was being shown that by looking at the good of that time, I could expect God to do the same. God used reframing to secure my emotions.

As I let go of the memory of fear and exchanged it for trusting God, reframing happened. My redemptive takeaway was: I can trust the Lord in this situation because of His unending faithfulness. The overwhelming fear began to fade.

The Lord offers all of us the opportunity to reclaim our past by revisiting past events. Saying yes to His invitation allows Him to use it for our good. We can offer an event from our past to the Lord and reframe it, knowing healing is coming. We walk away from that time, freed from the past.

In *Telling Secrets*, Frederick Buechner explains how God brings healing from our past. "The sad things that happened long ago will always remain part of who we are just as the glad and gracious things will too, but instead of being a burden of guilt, recrimination, and regret that make us constantly stumble as we go, even the saddest things can become, once we have made peace with them, a source of wisdom and strength for the journey that still lies ahead. It is through memory that we are able to reclaim much of our lives that we have long since written off by finding that in everything that has happened to us over the years God was offering us possibilities of new life and healing which, though we may have missed them at the time, we can still choose and be brought to life by and healed by all these years later."[5]

Separate the situation from the story

The goal of separating the situation from the story, as Vivian Gornick named these aspects, is to consider it in a new light. Going back after time has passed helps us to construct an understanding of the situation that couldn't have been possible at the time. Reframing a situation allows us to emerge from adverse circumstances with an ability to overcome, adapt and find new strength. It doesn't mean that what was bad becomes good. It means we can see the good that comes from it. The situation hasn't changed, but our perspective of it has. We are not the same person we were when the event took place. Now we are able to form new takeaways.

Reframing a situation allows us to emerge from adverse circumstances with an ability to overcome, adapt and find new strength.

My takeaway is my overarching theme about what happened. Something I may have never noticed before can present itself now. New perspectives about my college accident may surprise me as I process that event. As I review the accident, I now see my accident as a way I grew from a first-time car owner and freshman student to a young woman who could navigate problems and issues that we all experience. I came away from it wanting to do things differently. I now understanding why people in traumatic situations can isolate and separate from others. I came away having to face the fact that I was changed through the event, but I also grew.

Just like the students in my classroom, when I separate the facts of an event, I can arrive at a place of grace and newly formed wisdom. I can pinpoint negative thoughts or beliefs associated with the event. I become aware of my part in the event. Any blame I have unduly put on myself can be discarded. I can choose to remove that guilt, any feelings of failure, or overwhelmingly negative perspectives. As the director of my story, I can focus on aspects that contribute to my growth, my resilience that I've gained, or any newfound wisdom. I can ask myself, what did I learn about myself and others? How can I move forward from the event?

As I integrate the reframed story into my understanding, I am choosing to have this positive take away as part of my memory. I am rewriting history, framing my experience in my present-day meaning. As I recall the rewritten event in the future, God will use this strategy with future situations.

I can reframe a traumatic situation and form truth about it that offers redemption and grace. I will have a renewed sense of confidence about any difficult situation that happens. I know I am not stuck in pain or bitterness. I will wait on the Lord and take His lead in reframing that event just as I did with other events. Instead of having bitterness, or anger, I am now framing it in a new story of redemptive truth that serves to move me forward with greater resilience.

Once we know the truth of our new takeaway, we can see beliefs being formed. We are affirming what scripture tells us about God making all things new. Van Norman underscores the redemptive process of reframing. "Once we know His truth clearly in these tender, messy, congested parts of our story, we will indeed be joyful and glad to hear that all of the painful, embarrassing, horrific moments of our past have been given voices to celebrate the one who permitted them to break us in the first place. Only in the honesty of our stories will we feel purged and clean, washed, and whiter than snow."[6]

His ways are healing

God highlights past events and then helps us to process them as an act of liberating us. He works to draw our hearts into specific areas of our past to heal us and connect intimately with us. He selects these events as we pay attention and as we hold fast to Him. His motivation in drawing our hearts to Him is to remove the burdens of the past.

"Behold, you delight in truth in the inward being, and you teach me wisdom in the secret heart. Purge me with hyssop, and I shall be clean; wash me, and I shall be whiter than snow. Let me hear joy and gladness; let the bones that you have broken rejoice." (Psalm 51:6-7, ESV) We know His ways are healing. We know His goal is our freedom.

After I process an event and reframe it with my takeaway, I see how grace and hope are actively working through me. His grace redefines and affirms me. I replaced the old negatives that were attached to the situation and instead will recall the new and redeemed statement of the grace and acceptance I long for. I speak it over this situation and over the people involved in it. As I receive His grace, there is renewed hope.

Truly God works all things together for my good, whether I can see that good or not. In Romans 6:4 we are reminded of the sacrifice that Jesus paid, making the way for our redemption. "We were buried therefore with him by baptism into death, in order that, just as Christ was raised from the dead by the glory of the Father, we too might walk in newness of life." He faithfully redeems our memories and heals the wounds that were connected to them.

The Lord offers all of us the opportunity to reclaim our past by revisiting past events. Saying yes to His invitation allows Him to use it for our good. He walks with us in our healing journey and because we trust Him, we go there with Him. He brings new insights, a change that strengthens relationships, or maybe offers a path for forgiveness. He offers us freedom from deep pain, renewed hope, transformed perspectives, and new identities. We can offer an event from our past to the Lord and reframe it, knowing healing is coming. He will bring us redemption in that process. We walk away freed from the past.

No exceptions

We sometimes carry wounds from our parents. Most people do. Sometimes we don't have the opportunity to restore a relationship before the person passes away. But a person's death does not mean my memories of them die. I can choose to bring healing into the stories that involve them. The truth of His grace and redemption still operates through me.

I, in fact, have two mothers. So reframing past hurts involving them was tricky. You see, my mothers were sisters. The younger sister was my biological mother, though I knew her as my aunt, and the older sister, I knew as my mother. The older sister and her husband adopted me when I was two. The three of them vowed together to never speak of it to me or the rest of the family. They told me I was adopted, but not who my biological mother was or what my origin was. As I grew older and asked too many questions, it became a bone of contention between my mother and myself. I felt my birth caused resentment and shame in her.

After I was twenty-three it all came out via a deep confession from my aunt. Because she had broken her vow of secrecy, anger and resentment changed their relationship, creating a break in the family. The sisters didn't meet for coffee in the mornings. My dad and my uncle didn't play golf on Wednesdays any more. Their secrets and the misunderstanding it formed in me created a sadness in me and alienation from my family.

Even though I had forgiven each of them individually, I knew when God put His finger on these wounds, I needed to address them from His perspective. Though I was never able to bring them together to talk and perhaps heal their relationship, I did have the responsibility to ask for healing of my wounds from it.

My adopted mother was in the throes of Alzheimer's when this reframing process began. I began by looking at my relationship with her and the hopes that were dashed by her broken relationship with her younger sister. I had prayed for reconciliation, for mended relationships, and for unity in our family for years. This was the first step: analyzing the situation. I call it the "before" step.

In the next step, the "during" step, God asked me what I had not forgiven either of them for during my formative years. I repented of my resentment and unresolved bitterness. This is when my perspective of the past had an opportunity to change. The Lord showed me their personal weaknesses, and I could see them as loving, but over-controlling, in how they handled my adoption and the secrets about my birth. This step helped me to receive their imperfect love as parents. It helped me to let go of the prayers for reconciliation that I knew I could not see this side of eternity. By the time I began working out these details with God, both my aunt and my mother had passed away. But the reframed relationship was alive and well and brought hope and peace in me.

The third step is "after." The result of this reframing process was a redemption of their memory and freedom for myself. Redemption operates through the faith and hope I have in Him. The story I now have of my family is the truth of a new takeaway.

Here is the redemption that has formed because of reframing the memory with my parents and my aunt: they were operating with the truth that they knew. In their attempt to control my future and my aunt's, they disregarded our needs. I forgive them. I accept that adverse decision and the wounds it created in a new and redemptive way.

Redemption operates through the faith and hope I have in Him.

I know that love takes many forms and sometimes causes pain for others. As a result, the first thought I have of them is love and acceptance instead of being a victim and tormented by the memory. As I move forward, I can actively love them when I think of them.

I can hold that relationship up to the Lord considering eternity. What hasn't been redeemed this side of heaven, will be accomplished, and restored as we live with Him there. I process the grief that I have about that loss.

I still hold onto the hope for restored relationships that I held onto during their lives. From time to time, I will grieve and long for that restoration. I lean into the Lord in my wounded state and apply His promise of wiping every tear away in eternity to heart. I surrender all those emotions to the One who knows me.

"After two decades of studying the brain, I can tell you that it's physiologically impossible to disconnect our identities from any person or experience in our past," Van Norman writes. "We are all intricately tied to one another and deeply marked by our experiences, big and small. God doesn't want to redefine our lives apart from our experiences, even the painful, shameful ones. Instead, he wants to tell us the truth about himself through others, our personalities, and the nonrandom sequence of events we call life."[7] This is the reason for our reframing. It is relevant to recall Philippians 2:13: "For it is God who works in you to will and to act in accordance with His good purpose."

God uses all our past for redeeming all of our hearts. Our reframed story can bring healing, forgiveness, and understanding. Through this redemptive act we see His hand in making all things new.

Our stories free us

Hearing a survivor's story impacts us, giving us hope. It demonstrates the power that lives in our stories. In journaling portions of my story, I sift through it, mining for truth. In reframing it, I learn something about myself. I learned who I was then and why I reacted the way I did. I see myself as I am now and how I can formulate a response bathed in grace and acceptance, that is different from the initial reaction. It is an act of redemption. We can become aware of the negativity that resulted from old thoughts about a situation. We can discard those beliefs.

As survivors in our stories, we observe our changing selves. We're no longer victims. Our story becomes a tool for our healing and empowerment. Recounting the situation helps us to find the meaning in it. It helps to make sense of it. When we work to reframe our stories, we free ourselves.

Our stories also help others to find meaning. One of the greatest benefits of reading about other survivors is to support the survivor that lives in all of us. We are told that surviving and thriving is possible. In telling our hard but valuable stories, we create hope and healing paths for many to follow. Telling our stories to others offers them the power we have gained. We retell it over time to amend and form personal truths that become part of our beliefs. Then we share it with others to offer them the same healing and hope that we have acquired.

TAKEAWAYS

- God leads us to revisit memories to draw us toward a redemptive takeaway.
- We can reframe a traumatic situation and form a story about it that offers redemption and grace.
- Our reframed story can bring healing, forgiveness, and understanding from difficult events and wounded relationships.
- We can become aware of the negativity that resulted from old thoughts about a situation and discard those beliefs.
- Recounting a past event helps us to find the meaning and to make sense of it.

SPIRITUAL PRACTICE: REFRAMING AN EVENT

Take your time in following the reframing process and applying it. Ask the Lord if there is a memory He wants you to reframe. When He makes you aware of it, journal your before, during, and after categories of that event or relationship.

Use your quiet times with Him to allow for any forgiveness, softening of heart, or unattended sin to be dealt with. Focus on scripture that points toward healing and redemption in Him. Write the reframed and redemptive perspective that you have developed.

CHAPTER 7
Failing Forward

This is what the past is for! Every experience God gives us, every person He puts in our lives is the perfect preparation for the future that only He can see.

—Corrie ten Boom[1]

I WAS SO EXCITED.

The church I'd belonged to for eight years had invited me to lead sixty students through an art curriculum that would support their spiritual journey. My mentor, a former board member at the church, wanted me to be a part of the leadership team for the course that would include that curriculum. I felt honored. The course would combine my passion for art and spiritual formation.

I had taught art, led groups, and ministered in prayer in different ways before. We made a plan: nine months of art curriculum, one session per month. And the Lord laid out a plan for a team member and I to pray for the students weekly. The sixty students were young and ready to deep dive into sharing life and dreaming big with the Lord. I was too.

But after just two months, the art portion of the class was dropped.

I only found out by seeing the third month's meeting agenda. My usual teaching portion of the meeting did not appear on the outline of the meeting.

After the second month of silence, I contacted the director and asked, "Are we proceeding as planned? What do I do for next month's meeting?"

Her terse reply offered no explanation. "I'm sorry you are having a problem with this."

What did the abrupt change mean? Had I failed? The Lord led me here. Didn't that ensure success? Had I failed Him? I had experience in what I was teaching. I am certified in leading art groups to promote personal growth. I had used art to record my journey with the Lord for years and mentored women to benefit spiritually from that practice. I taught art from kindergarten to high school for years.

However, I knew my experience wouldn't keep me from making mistakes. But in making them, couldn't I learn from them? Communication could have created a path toward that. But it didn't happen. I felt betrayed.

After this pattern of silent dismissal continued, I knew that I couldn't continue. But instead of backing down from the position, I felt that quitting would be irresponsible. I continued with prayer support and in making materials available during retreats. I decided I would wait until the end of the course and then resign. Even if I didn't understand why the plans had abruptly changed, I believed that in time, I would hear from the Lord. God would give me His perspective.

You may have done this. You want to serve, have something to give and believe in the vision and the people. You volunteer, set up a schedule, get training, and get on board. After all, when you have done this before, you may not be expecting difficulty or something different than what you felt God's plan included? For me, the shift in plans challenged my ability to trust God. It required me to blindly follow the changes without understanding. I thought perhaps in time, I would be able to have a better perspective and some understanding. I held on in faith.

It was May and time for the retreat. I planned to help where extra hands were needed. Retreats provide deep spiritual growth. This one held power, prayer and laughter. Until the last day. It was one of those moments frozen in time.

"You don't trust anyone…"

On the final morning of the retreat, I sipped my tea after breakfast as I chatted with a friend in a group of about twenty of the leadership team. The pastor stood a few people away from me and out of nowhere, called me out.

Everyone stopped their conversations and leaned in to hear him. "You do not trust anyone." The air was still. He paused. In my mind I answered, "But I trust you." I couldn't speak. He continued, "Maybe it's because of the wounds you received from churches in the past. Maybe…" My heart pounded loudly, my knees felt unsteady.

I knew he was still talking, but I couldn't hear him. His voice faded as though I had been transported to the opposite corner of the room. I smiled robotically. Then it was over. No closure or clarification.

The group split into couples, everyone depositing a coffee mug in the sink and quietly making their way out. My brain was awash in white. I was shaking. I walked back to my dorm room, my eyes focused on each step. I lay down. "God, what just happened?' Why had he said those things? None of them were true. Why had he called me out in front of the team?"

I had one thought. I need clarity. It would be months before I had a chance to seek it.

Just as I had planned, I had resigned my position with the team. I felt the way to move forward was to seek to understand what had happened at the retreat. It took months of counseling to get me to the point where I could deal with my feelings, my words and my questions. I needed to talk with my pastor, but I didn't know how. If I spoke honestly, what would happen? Would God make a way for understanding between us? Would there be forgiveness and restoration?

Months later we met. We had some small talk, and I began. "Can I ask you what you were trying to say to me at the end of the retreat?"

He didn't recall. "I was embarrassed and humiliated," I said. "When you said that I didn't trust anyone, I was stunned. Because I trusted you. No, I have not been wounded by the church. I, I, I..." I stopped talking. He grimaced and looked out the window. I knew I had already said too much. Or maybe I had said it wrong. He seemed angry but only said that I had waited too long to talk to him about it. I was immediately sad and regretful. Tears came from nowhere. He made a slight nod. He got up to leave. And then as he walked away, he said, "I'm sorry."

When you feel betrayed

I wanted to believe the best about those who were involved in this season. I had walked through reconciliation in the past and seen how the Lord brought understanding and forgiveness. Because of this, I had confidence that reconciliation would be the outcome of our meeting. I believed we could resolve misunderstandings and move forward. When that didn't happen, I began to distrust leadership. My hopes of receiving healing from the ones who were there to support healing were dashed.

I want you to know that if you feel betrayed by an organization, whether that be by a non-profit, school, church or business, God is there to heal your heart and provide ways to move forward. After a tumultuous shift from trust to distrust, our world can feel unhinged. It may seem as though we are bound to the struggle and unable to move forward until the other party involved says or does the right thing. It can feel as though our world is on tilt until the pain stops. But our healing may not be in the hands of the ones who caused it. God makes a way for healing deep heart wounds that can detour around another's involvement. He can redeem difficult issues without it happening the way we feel it should. No matter the circumstance, our first steps toward healing are our responsibility. To seek Him in all things means that when we are betrayed, we still can choose God's way through the pain to healing, freedom, and clarity.

No matter what others chose to do or not do, I still knew that forgiveness was the first step in gaining healing. However, I didn't base forgiveness on my feelings. Though I still felt the pain, I began what I will call "a blind walk into an undiscovered country." I kept hearing the Lord say He was taking me to this "undiscovered country," so I knew if that was the case, I would follow Him. I put His words in Luke 6:37 before me: "...Forgive, and you will be forgiven." Without knowing how to forgive by faith, I still chose to do that.

I couldn't know what was in the hearts and minds of those who chose to do and say things that were painful. But I could trust God to bring something good from forgiving by faith. I believed that He would bring something good because He is good. While my fractured emotions were screaming for help, I chose to take God's hand and let go of my need to "right all the wrongs." My emotions would have to take the back seat. I knew God was piloting the way and would heal my emotions if I stayed beside Him.

I wrestled with two painful questions as I processed this pain before the Lord. They both raised their ugly heads as I worked out my salvation in fear and trembling in this "undiscovered country." They were: can I trust those in the church? And the second one tied to it, can I move forward after failing?

I wanted to make sense of it all: the art course deletion, being called out, and then not having closure or forgiveness. Pain and confusion filled every quiet time I had. How would God lead me to healing and wholeness through this jungle of emotions? I looked for Him in His Word and in prayer. I sought wisdom and counsel from those who were closest to me. I took responsibility where I could. I wanted the Lord to give me courage and hope to move forward. How could He use what felt like an epic failure?

I am failing, not a failure

For many of us, failure is simply the opposite of success. It is black or white, one or the other. If you don't succeed, you call that failure. Maybe, on the other hand, after experiencing years of success and failure, you have come to see failure as an opportunity to look at yourself in the mirror. You realize it holds personal information about the responsibility you have in a situation. Failure can provide an opportunity to learn what the Lord wants to say about our character. In God's hands failure becomes a way to gain wisdom. The Lord uses your openness to His instruction to bring redemption to the loss and heals your heart.

The Bible says our success is tied to our actions. "Commit your actions to the Lord, and your plans will succeed." (Proverbs 16:3, NLT) The Bible also speaks of fruitfulness as a sign of success. "For those whose delight is in His law," Psalm 1:3 says, that person "is like a tree planted by streams of water, which *yields its fruit in season* and whose leaf does not wither—whatever they do prospers." (AMP) Success depends on actions, plans, and the process of our own character being built. This verse points to something being grown in us over time. As we continue with Him in relationship, His living waters of truth will yield spiritual fruit in us. Failure can produce spiritual fruitfulness as we wait on God to reveal His purposes.

Examining personal failure starts from a desire to learn what life is teaching us through circumstances.

Does God prevent failure? Does He have a reason for putting us in situations that then fail? What can we expect as redemption from Him when failing brings discouragement?

Humans are built to search for meaning. Examining personal failure starts from a desire to learn what life is teaching us through circumstances. We are built to find meaning in stories, in life, and in our finding our purpose. My immediate reaction was trying to learn what went wrong with the course plan. My mind went from what went wrong, to what did I do wrong?

When we are reeling from self-doubt it is difficult to find meaning.

It can feel like being lost in a dense forest. Our emotions can keep us from seeing the path forward. Walking through difficult seasons of extracting truth from failure is much the same. We can't see the forest because of the thickness of the emotions surrounding us. Recently I was hiking in the beautiful foothills surrounding our valley. This trail wove through thick groves of oak, cedar, and pine trees. After the trail twisted and turned, I could not see where we had come from or where we were headed. In much the same way our emotions keep us from seeing the way to move forward. When we process our emotions, holding fast to God's lead, the way becomes clear. Gaining wisdom from failure takes time. Processing our emotions and thoughts with Him develops trust and faith in Him.

As we grieve, however, we do so with hope in His purposes for us. He is offering truth that will soon bring life and light. In time, if we continue to follow Him, the scenery on the trail will change. The trees of confusion and misunderstanding will separate, and we will have a newly found truth. When our emotions calm, we are more able to receive His insight. Meaning and purpose will come. All in time. We can link reasons and meaning to problems and setbacks which help form the path in moving forward. He will bring perspective that couldn't have been discovered any other way.

Jay Wolf writes: "We don't have to look far in the Bible to see that it's almost comically overflowing with stories of people who failed badly, yet whom God not only loved but chose to be integral parts of His story of love in the world."[2]

Just read the stories of Adam and Eve, Abraham, Noah, Moses, David, James and John, Peter, and Martha. And yet, we learn from their stories that failing did not stop them from trusting God with their lives. In fact, Noah, Abraham, Moses, David are also listed in Hebrews 11:7-32, as those who walked in great faith.

By showing us their vulnerabilities, God is teaching us about ours. We learn about trust, about our human tendencies toward sin, about the need to give and receive forgiveness. Through their lives we learn how to continue walking with God. As we follow the Lord, despite how uncertain our own strength may appear, or how painful the experience is, the Lord is strengthening our relationship with Him. In time, we can see His leading and how He uses circumstances to form our character through these situations.

This formation of resilient faith will happen as we hold fast to God while navigating through personal failure and let Him transform us in the process. He encourages us: "The Lord directs the steps of the godly. He delights in every detail of their lives. Though they stumble, they will never fall, for the Lord holds them by the hand." (Psalm 37: 23-24, NLT)

Faithfulness is obedience

Success from God's perspective is faithfulness. It is the result of our continuing in faith, the fruit of the Spirit, as He works in our lives. (see Galatians 5:22-23) Faithfulness requires me to continue with Him and receive truth from mistakes, from confessing sin, and from failure. We learn, operate in forgiveness, and move on as He leads us. It doesn't mean we forget, however. I acquire wisdom from my failures. To learn from them I need to forgive those whose missteps, weaknesses, or sins have impacted me. I will need to forgive myself for my responsibility in it. It's good to keep in mind that to fail is human. God uses imperfect people like you and me to achieve His purposes.

If failure causes regret and bitterness, it becomes difficult to attempt something new or risk again. Fear can remind us of what happened before. To use a baseball analogy, only those at bat have an opportunity to hit the ball. Our ability to continue in faith and obedience will depend on our saying yes by faith and to step up to our turn at bat again and again. And yet, not all our at bats will be home runs. Some will be outs. By obeying God, we are trusting Him over our trust in our ability to succeed. We trust Him despite our fear.

As I transverse the layers of my issues about failure, I am reminded again and again that there's fruitfulness in this process. Marva Dawn, theologian and educator, reflects on these benefits in her book, *The Sense of the Call.* "We actually derive great benefits from standing steadfast in ministries that are not in season." In her reference to ministry not being "in season," she means that it isn't popular or applauded. She continues, "To fulfill our calling even when it isn't wanted forces us to be sure of what we're doing. It drives us to our knees in prayer, in attentive listening, in humility. Then we're also released from the scramble for human approval and can do our work solely to please God."[3] Humility is that beautiful but rare fruit of the Spirit we all need. A dear friend recently told me that humility is the currency of God's kingdom. Walking with God through seasons of failure is one way we gain humility.

The prevailing question I had before the Lord during the months of failure in my story was: why had God led me into a situation that involved so much confusion and pain? Initially I felt I had read Him wrong in joining the leadership team. But when I traced back the confirmations over the previous summer, I knew that I hadn't. That meant He had a purpose for my walking through this epic failure.

Fear of failure

I grew up in a home that attached self-worth to achievement. I took dance, joined the girls' intramural team, and ran for student government. I reveled in succeeding. My parents felt that if I had the desire, they would help me participate in anything and everything. They did not think that adding more activities could be overwhelming or that ramping up a weekly schedule could make life exhausting. That wasn't a trending thought at that time. Nope! We were just living life.

My parents were hard workers. They gardened for six months, and canned and filled the freezer for the remaining six. They served meals to those in need, supported most church functions, taught Sunday School and were at Wednesday night prayer meetings. No harm, no foul. Except my talented mom would run herself ragged in serving. Her projects were massive undertakings: sewing formals, full-length coats, and fashionable outfits for me, and crocheting, macrame, and knitting sweaters for church bazaars. Painting and ceramics in her free time. Flower arranging for the pulpit on Sundays. She was busy, industrious, and skillful. She served in the after-school program, the missions project, and the church community center. Her weariness at times turned to anger. In the wee hours I would find her in the living room crying. She was tired. But she did not know how to say no. Her talents were in demand and made her who she was. Or did they?

I came to believe that what I did is viscerally linked to who I am. And maybe, it is a slippery slope for all of us. We become the roles we fill, and we think we are those jobs, those positions, or those titles. Those roles can then easily become enmeshed with our identities. Who I am can seem equal to what I do. Rebecca Lyons, in *Resilient Life*, puts it this way. "There's a fine line we cross where our work becomes our worth. This is true whether it's your vocation or the work of being the perfect role at home. It's so subtle, invisible even, that you rarely see it when it happens."[4] The desire to become like Him fades when we focus on something else. Our achievements can become an idol, something that drives us. Accomplishment and success can readily be a motivating force in serving the Lord.

After resigning from leadership, I felt empty. Because I was focused on the ministry when my position there ended, I saw it as an end in being able to minister at all. Instead of it being another step in following Him, I felt I had failed Him because I had not been able to accomplish what He led me to do. But this is not where the Lord was taking me. It was not the end of the story.

It took close to a year of seeking healing before I arrived at a place of acceptance and experienced periods of peace. But I still wondered why I continued to feel like a failure. That's when something happened that took my breath away. It has an intricate back story, so hang with me.

Meaning and purpose

My father, like many of his generation, fought bravely in WWII, but I never heard him talk about his battlefield experiences. Years later, I learned he had commanded a division in a strategic initiative in the Pacific Theater, earning several medals for his heroism. He went on to fight in the Korean War, where he was severely wounded. He spent his

last years in the military in charge of a supply post. He was disheart-
ened by this assignment. I think he may have felt like a failure.

Nearly a year and a half after my leadership resignation, I was
driving to an appointment. Out of nowhere, the Lord started stirring
memories of my father's internal struggles during that less than desir-
able supply post. He was once a decorated officer who led troops to a
victorious outcome. Now he handed out supplies and kept lists of
materials. His last position in his military career was less than equal to
his abilities. Instead of glory, he had a distinct sense of personal defeat.

Then, the Lord proposed a question: was your father the same man
in this menial supply position as he was as a leader in battle? Yes, Lord.
Yes. He was always that man. Always a hero and a godly man of
wisdom. Yes. Then the light turned, and the Lord flipped the script. "It
is the same for you. No matter what you do, how you serve or minister,
or don't serve, you are the same person to Me. I have invested Myself in
you. You are mine. You are the same to me no matter what you do."

In the time it took to steer into the turn lane, the Lord used my
father's situation to reveal His redemptive purpose in my failing
season. As I sat there, I could feel my dad's pain and understand his
self-doubt. Then the light changed, as tears filled my eyes, nearly
blinding me. I pulled off the road and let the Lord's words wash over
me. "This is who you are to Me. No matter what you do." He began to
describe who I am to Him. I soaked in the love of His words. My worth
did not depend on what I did. Achievement and success did not prove
my identity. My value was secure in Him because I belong to Him. His
gracious words brought purpose and meaning to the discouragement
and anxiety I had felt. He was removing my dependance on performance. Those words became my takeaway from the season of failure,
as well as my redemption in every future failure and in every difficulty
I would face.

Moving forward

You may not have an anxiety-filled season of failure. Yours may be
a failed test or a promotion that you didn't receive. Your failings may

be a slip in comparison. There are many ways we can feel like a failure. When there is a prevailing sense of guilt because your adult child has an on-going addiction. Or when a long-term relationship ends suddenly without closure. The details and severity may vary, but the process of finding God's perspective and receiving wisdom from Him afterwards is the same. We deal with our emotions in His Presence. We wait on Him, get His wise counsel, and walk forward with Him. We grow from these seasons and so does our resilience. Finding purpose and growing from the wisdom found in failing gives us courage to face whatever challenges lie ahead. Rather than expecting perfection from ourselves, we choose obedience to Him, knowing that is how God accomplishes His purposes.

If you feel alienated by hurt from people in an organization, please know God is with you. You are not alone. It can feel like there is nowhere to turn. You may feel the injustice of being one person facing a system within a church, school, or business. You must weigh the choices of how to forgive, manage your emotions as you process them, and receive God's strength to persevere as He heals your heart. You may decide to work with those that caused the pain and attend to the situation, seeking to bring a course correction to your organization. On the other hand, you may need space and time to simply heal and seek His direction. You may be asking yourself what's the next step in seeking a new job, finding a counselor, and choosing who to trust with your story. Know that God will go before you as you journey through it all. Whatever the betrayals are and no matter how deeply they have wounded your heart, God will make a way to bring trust and hope to you again.

Moving forward from these difficulties means choosing not to allow bitterness to work its way into your heart. Hear me. If left on its own, pain has a way of festering much like an infected wound. If you leave your pain unresolved or stuff it beneath a facade of denial, pretending that all is well, your pain will grow. Without care and protection of counsel and prayer, the infection will spread, traveling throughout the body. Over time bitterness created from these unre-solved emotions can cause more hurt to you than the wound itself. It can become a source of stress and anxiety, leading to physical problems. Wounds of unattended emotions can create deep-seeded bitterness that instead of healing, will multiply. If they are rehearsed in our heads or nonchalantly discussed, they will reproduce and sow discord in others. The goal is to extinguish the bitterness and heal before it can form.

If we allow God's love into these wounds, healing will come. By opening ourselves to God's truth and goodness these wounds will be cleansed. He will attend to the pain as only He can do. He will provide you with the truth and mercy your heart needs. Over time He will restore hope and move you toward an "undiscovered country," where you can live strong in His strength and mature from the distance you've traveled with Him to get there. His surgical handiwork will reform your life.

Psalm 84:6-7 describes this journey as being filled with God's promise: "Blessed are those whose strength is in you, whose hearts are set on pilgrimage. As they pass through the Valley of Baka, (the Amplified Version and New Living Translation refer to this as the "Valley of Weeping"), they make it a place of springs; the autumn rains also cover it with pools. They go from strength to strength, till each appears before God in Zion."

On this journey, those tear-producing struggles in time become a "place of springs," a place of refreshment. Healing is promised to us in the form of God's strength. We are told that we can go from "strength to strength." Our bending from the weight of the struggles forms resilient faith that cannot be broken. Can it be more rewarding or hopeful?

Purpose from the pain

Waiting for the Lord to give meaning and purpose to our failing is like finding hidden treasure in secret places. Just as it says in Isaiah 45:3, "I will give you hidden treasures, riches stored in secret places, so that you may know that I am the Lord, the God of Israel, who summons you by name." Our treasure is stored up for us by the Lord on the very paths we may not have chosen for ourselves. Places that I would not have gone otherwise is exactly where He stores the finest treasures. The best I could tell myself was this: everything that I knew was once unknown. So if Jesus led me into the unknown place that I found myself in, it's His desire for me to know Him there.

What I received as insight from this season was mind blowing. Most importantly it held freedom. My covenant commitment to serve Him was not broken. But I could see how achievement was threatening God's rightful place in me. My allegiance to God was being compromised because I so valued having a role. Did I need to have a role in church ministry to feel I had value? And why was it a shock that something I created was not received? That the course was deleted? Why was it so devastating to see people I trusted not follow through? There were lessons for my future in all of this.

What I had experienced was refining my heart. It tested me but He held me while we walked through it together. Now I understood how God saw me. I had read it in scripture, but now I had heard Him tell me, "This is who you are to me." His truth filled a void that I didn't know was there. I no longer needed to achieve to have value. My worth was no longer attached to winning, achieving, succeeding, or operating in a certain role. I trusted God's promise: "I am my Beloved's and my Beloved is mine." (Song of Solomon 6:3)

I learned that I can trust Him despite not understanding where He's leading me or why. What changed for me? I began working one on one with students as they finished the discipleship program. I shifted the time I had spent in church involvement and instead, sowed time and energy into relationships. I wrote and created art as a vehicle of expressing His glory. I learned again that God's ways are active and operating even and especially when I don't sense them or understand them.

It took time to walk through the season of perceived failure. It took perseverance when I was in pain and weighed down by discouragement and self-doubt. I had been through adversity and crisis before. But during this time, I felt like I had failed the Lord, my church, and myself. It was one of the darkest periods I had known. I did not find quick answers. The season was not easy or comfortable. It challenged my faith. But God was there. He was using what I couldn't make sense of for my good. I was decreasing while His will and sovereignty in my life were increasing. (See John 3:30)

Because of this season I learned about our frailties as humans; my weaknesses and those of others. I became aware that two contrasting things can be true at one time. I can feel great disappointment in the outcomes of trusting God and yet, at the same time, I can experience the fruit of the struggle: redemption and hard-fought change. I can discern harsh truths about myself in caring too much for accomplishment and not see how God is using that truth. I became aware that I can take steps toward restoration but release any expectations about the outcome. People require forgiveness, acceptance, and grace. In forgiving others, and in their forgiving me, I also hold these two truths in tension: they are used by God and at the same time, are fallible. So am I. Thank you God for the grace to accept both of these facts.

Proverbs 24:16 says it best: "For a righteous man falls seven times, and rises again." (AMP) Our numerous falls and failures move us to rise just one more time than we fall. That rising is an act of our will and an act of God's redemptive work in us. When it happens in the future, we can be reminded of the seven-time reference here. In scripture seven times simply means, it will happen again and again. God will redeem our failings and fallings again and again and again. In those experiences, resilient faith is given space, opportunity, and grace to enlarge, grow, and be greater than it was before.

God promises us in John 10:10 that He is giving us abundant life. "I have come that they may have life and have it abundantly." Some of us interpret that promise to mean we are never to experience discouragement, problems, trauma from these issues, difficulty, adversity, or failure. But a few chapters later, Jesus provides a counterintuitive perspective when He says: "In this world you will have trouble." We don't need faith to agree with that one, do we? In our trouble, He will be with us. He is with us in the missteps, the accidents, and the failures. We repent of our sin, and He forgives and cleanses us. That's what makes the difference; because He has gone before us, He knows the reason for our facing and walking through failure. "I have told you these things," Jesus adds, "so that in Me you may have peace. In this world you will have trouble. But take heart! I have overcome the world." (John 16:33)

Author and pastor John Maxwell writes, "Everything in life brings risk. It's true that you risk failure if you try something bold because you might miss it. But you also risk failure if you stand still and don't try anything new. The less you venture out, the greater your risk of failure. Ironically the more you risk failure—and actually fail—the greater your chances of success."[5]

We become aware that we are bending as we struggle, but our faith is not breaking. Indeed, God is making us into something new.

Failure doesn't stop us. It keeps us informed about our hearts, our skills, and our self-worth. It teaches us to move forward with God despite the fear, anxiety or discouragement. God provides us opportunities to follow Him down life's winding roads even when they are unfamiliar or uncomfortable. Even when it has been painful and difficult, in time, we see the fruit of the changes we are making. We become aware that we are bending as we struggle, but our faith is not breaking. Indeed, God is making us into something new. We are His and we journey with Him in finding meaning even in failure. It is a worthy venture. We learn to trust Him even more as He reveals purpose in how He has used the pain. We learn to lean hard on Him. Because of God's life-altering love, we move forward with a more resilient faith as Paul's words in Philippians 3:13-14 encourage us: "Forgetting what is behind and straining toward what is ahead, I press on toward the goal to win the prize for which God has called me heavenward in Christ Jesus."

TAKEAWAYS

- God uses failure as a mirror into our hearts.
- Gaining wisdom from failure takes time. Processing emotions and our thoughts with Him develops trust and faith in Him.
- Failure can produce spiritual fruitfulness as we wait on God to reveal His purposes.
- God does not waste the pain and suffering we go through when we fail. He has meaning and purpose for it all.
- Resilient faith is formed as we continue to hold fast to God while navigating through personal failure.

SPIRITUAL PRACTICE: IMAGINATIVE PRAYER

Your imagination (that is, your ability to picture something in your head) is a gift from God, which we can use to connect with God. Begin by sitting quietly. Ask God to guide your thoughts. Then respond to the following prompts by drawing images or journaling.

Imagine your current spiritual state as a weather event. Are you in a lush garden filled with radiant and soothing sunlight? Or is there a storm continuing and you just want to find the way through? Draw or write what's in your mind's eye. Pray as the Lord reveals His presence in your current weather environment.

Do you feel his peace in the storm? His blessing in the sunshine? No matter what you're facing, God is with you. We cannot change our circumstances, but we can choose to focus on God's presence. What do you need from God to feel safe and connected? What questions can you ask Him about where you are and what you're facing?

CHAPTER 8
Going the Distance

Let us rid ourselves of every burden and sin that clings to us
and persevere in running the race that lies before us...

—Hebrews 12:1

THERE IS nothing on earth created for distance running like a human
being. There are faster animals: the cheetah, the gazelle, or the horse.
Even a dog can outrun a human. But nothing can keep on running,
logging mile after mile like we can. Long after animals have quit,
humans endure. We were made for endurance. I believe our bodies
hold the truth about persevering long after we have felt the pressure is
too much to continue. Physically we were made for getting back up,
again and again, and going the distance with the Lord. He created us to
endure.

We are made in His image, and He does not give in, give up, or let
go. Our nature, when conformed to His, is to persist in doing good, to
rise after failing, to hold on in hope, and to never give up. The survival
instinct has a purpose, to keep us steady when everything looks like it's
falling apart. Our will to survive can be seen in the runner's focus for
the finish line, the biker headed up a mountain, the woman nursing

her newborn baby, and in her child as he's learning to take his first steps. We were created to go the distance. We were made to endure.

When we continue to persist, we prove that perseverance is alive and well, living in us. We prove that His nature to persevere is deeply rooted in us, as we are tested, strengthened, or fall and get back up. Then we dig deep into our convictions, lean hard into the Lord for His grace and begin it all again. Belonging to Him means transformation takes place as we continue. We are given the promise that Christ who began a good work in you WILL carry it on to completion. (See Philippians 1:6)

For the sake of going the distance and accomplishing this transformation, He has given you a desire to be faithful. Resilience is His nature. Resilience becomes ours, because we are made in His image, and are growing in Christlikeness. Our lives become a testimony to going the distance.

The strategies, stories, and encouragement provided in these chapters offer you a plan to use in your life. Whether you are in the thick of hardships or just need to gather scriptural promises to fuel your day, you can return to these pages to reaffirm what God says about who you are and then use that identity to follow Him. When you need to throw off the lies that can come against you and instead, renew your mind, you are building ways to move forward. When confronted with a past that casts you in a discouraging light, you can reframe that situation and take the director's chair. You can form a different story. As you look at failure with a new perspective you can form a better takeaway by seeing what was gained.

Now you're equipped with ways to get back up one fall at a time, to gain strength daily from leaning into His presence in the Word. Now prayer and community are not rote habits but instead provide you with authentic ways to seek God and reach out to others. Now you fight against the demise of continuing hardships by looking to Him to restore you, even as those challenges unfold. He has promised it to you. Now you are willing to wait on Him for answers and guidance that will surely come. He is with you and for you. Now you can slow down to catch up to Him.

When I experienced the magnitude of the thyroid cancer with my most recent recurrence, it left me speechless. I couldn't quite understand it. "Repeat that again," I said to my Harvard-graduated oncologist. He clarified the facts: "Periodic scans will keep you alive, but you will always have minuscule cancer cells growing in your body." Here is the clincher. To ensure slow growth of these cells I would be kept in a medically induced state of hyperthyroidism. For life.

My response to these facts is crucial to how I relate to God, live my life, and how I think. My mindset will determine what choices I make. If I see medically induced hyperthyroidism as *the* predictor of how I can live, it can negatively short-circuit my ability to "live, move, and have my being" dictated by Him. (Acts 17:28, AMP) But if I can properly put the diagnosis beneath the wings of almighty God, then I am free to be drawn by Him. I will use wisdom in modifying activity when my energy is low, but I am not allowing my mind to be controlled by that singular physical issue.

Here is where surrender and waiting on God work together. Instead of being a victim of the situation, I am free to respond to God and see my future with expectation. I can thrive despite what I am living with. God will bring life to me as I look to Him to be the source for anticipating good in the land of the living. I align with Him as I surrender to His timetable of bringing that goodness. This relieves stress because I am living on His grace, not my fallible abilities. I live life in tandem with Him. My expectancy of His goodness is what dictates my choices. Living in possibilities that are grounded in Him opens up pathways to experience Him. My expectancy of Him bringing goodness carves a pathway for Him to move.

The prayer of relinquishment is a necessary routine for those of us needing to let go of our situation on a regular basis. We can call it letting go or surrendering our will. It can be something we use as we face the day or a prayer we turn to when we see ourselves trying to take back control.

I don't provide that prayer as a list of things to do to move God's heart and get answers. We cannot simply say to ourselves, "If this happens, do that." Just the opposite. Everyone's journey with God is different. But He does have a process and a purpose for our waiting on Him.

Your path of following God as you wait will have certain signposts. You have learned that He directs you in ways you have encountered before. Perhaps He wakes you in the middle of the night when you face a big decision. Maybe He consistently offers you truth from a well-worn devotional. God might direct you to a chapter and verse that speaks directly to your exact circumstances. These will be yours to discover as you wait on Him. He creates a unique relationship for each one of us. These are beautiful and varied. But relinquishing our desires is foundational for all of us in learning how to wait with God.

His greatest feat

The story of Gary Miracle is just that, a miracle. I first learned of Gary in Harris Faulkner's book *Faith Still Moves Mountains*.[1] At thirty-eight he had already accomplished the life of which he had dreamed. He was a digital marketer who could work from home, which allowed him to coach all four of his boys, ages five through fifteen.

But all that changed in the blink of an eye when Gary went into septic shock after complications from the flu. In the days that followed he survived his heart stopping, a coma, and severe loss of oxygen to his limbs. After ten days, Gary woke up, but his arms and legs were the color of coal. Because of the loss of oxygen, all four limbs had to be amputated.

How would he respond? As a believer, Gary was drawn to the story of Job. Job was an unlikely hero who, though he obeyed God, lost everything in his life. Gary admired Job's faith to believe in God's goodness despite his loss. "I had spent my life telling people and preaching that God was good," he explained. "Now that something traumatic happened in my life, was I going to live like God wasn't good?" Gary set his sights on walking with God in the challenges that lay ahead. He knew this would be the greatest feat of his life. With God's help, he would make it.

In the next season, he and his family learned to receive support and assistance from health care workers, family, friends, and the church. They helped him navigate the hall in a motorized chair. They encouraged him as he learned to use prosthetics. In time he became functional again.

Then the call came for him to be featured in a video. Gary's good friends in the group, Mercy Me, had written a song, "Say I Won't," to honor him. Gary used his newly found functionality to give glory to God. His life had vastly changed. But his faith had only grown. As the line in the song says, "So keep on saying I won't/And I'll keep proving you wrong."[2]

This is what resilience is. Bending and not breaking when life seems impossible. Saying yes when everything in us recoils in a loud, "No!" It is confronting impossibility with the possibilities that God offers us.

Holding on to God

What made the difference for Gary Miracle? Was it the support he had throughout his ordeal? Was it an abundance of faith? He would probably say that all these things helped. But his decision was between him and God. At the point that he knew that he was going to lose his limbs, God had already planted the seed of hope. Gary remembered his thoughts about Job and how he relied on God's goodness. Of all the characters to draw hope from, Job seems the least likely to create a life-raft of faith around. But Gary followed his hero and focused on the goodness of God. He decided to hold on to God. That made all the difference.

The truth is, when I'm going through a battle and I make a decision to hold on to God, that's when I begin to receive strength from Him. Those decisions to say "yes'" to God fuel us to move forward. What if you don't hold on? What if the pressure is too much, the trial too hard, the cost too great to sacrifice? Even in your bleakest sin, in your darkest failures, in your embarrassing doubts, God is with you and for you. One turn toward Him can change your path. Reach out and take Him at His word. Open the Bible and allow your heart to receive grace and mercy. Then forgive yourself, because He is forgiving you, even as you are asking Him for that forgiveness.

Though our struggles are vastly different from Gary Miracle's, we have the same responsibility and decisions to make when facing a crisis. We confront the choice to move forward with God or collapse in our doubt and discouragement. In saying yes to Him, we bring the opportunity for miraculous stories to our lives.

In our weakest seasons, there is hope. God brings restoration when we cannot find a way back from doubt. He will lay down a bridge connecting us with Him. Hope is not lost after a fall. God will renew your purposes and restore life. You will reemerge. God and His life for you is greater than a human mind can fathom. His love will cause you to rise again. You may have fallen, but His love will not let you stay there. Resilience is being built as you make that determined decision to let God love you.

Even when we feel like we cannot hold on, He is always holding on to us. We teach ourselves to submit the circumstances to Him and not let go. We choose to believe that His goodness will make a way for our lives. That doesn't mean we are perfect in it. We are human and do very human things. When the struggle is too much, we can slip, forget what's important, and fail in our commitment to Him. We can depart from faith. We can allow ourselves to be easily distracted with the weight of overwhelming circumstances. We can choose to let go, doubt, or even walk away.

Or, you can choose to be faithful, to obey, and to trust. You can declare in the middle of a disastrous season: "I'm here, God! I'm right here with You! I'm not going anywhere!" No matter what we are going through or the duration of that crisis, we make these declarations of faith. "I am holding on to You by an act of my will."

In those small and large ways, you have been faithful. No one sees it all. But He does. Through these steps, you are being built with His strength. You are realizing a resiliency you may have not had before. You've learned during these hard, harsh times that God has been very intentional about directing you. You've waited on Him, and no one knows how hard it's been. But He has led you through it and you have followed. By walking with Him in life's hardest season He has taught you to persevere.

You hold on to God because of His goodness. He is not an idea or a positive mantra. He is not only your human-centered thoughts about Him. He is the author and creator of life and love. He is who we need for any crisis that comes our way. He is faithful and true to you. You know Him because scriptures describe His love. Then you experience the validity of what they tell you. Through the crisis and the hardships, you discover that what the Bible says about God is for your rescue in times of loss, discouragement, and anxiety. You find the height, the depth, and the width of His love when difficulties mount.

As hardships continue and you need more of Him than the previous day, then you find Him able to fill you with more of His love. You cannot know the love of God unless you take hold of it, seek Him, and take Him to heart. It is during your greatest times of crisis that you will find His love satisfies, strengthens, and fills you. To hold on to Him when difficulties are mounting is faith in action. This is resilient faith being built in you.

Continuing in faithfulness

Are you familiar with the parable of the Ten Virgins, a parable recorded in Matthew 25:1-13? If you are, you may have had to pause after reading it. It can seem overwhelming. You can come away with a defeatist perspective of feeling like you can never be enough and feel like giving up. Or, you may have the opposite reaction. It may inspire you to try every way humanly possible to go the distance, in frantic effort. It's even easy to think the poor virgins tried but just fell asleep and missed Christ's return and wonder what hope you have. But I'd like to propose an alternative takeaway.

In Jesus' parable, the ten virgins are separated into two groups, one that is prepared for the bridegroom and the second that is not. The first group's preparation kept them ready for His return. Their constant readiness made them available at a moment's notice. They "took oil in jars along with their lamps," verse 4. Their focus never left the need for preparation. In applying this truth, we can ask ourselves about the plan we have made to go the distance with the Lord in our lives.

We persevere by continuing in faithfulness to God. We cannot be strong, have passion, and do all the do's all the time. But we can receive God's fresh oil of grace, hope, and faith daily. Today is the day we focus on. We stay prepared with our jars filled, with the virgins that make it, as we walk with the Lord *today*. Hebrews 10:23 states: "Let us hold fast the confession of our hope without wavering, for He who promised is faithful." (ESV) We keep our eyes focused on Jesus, living faithful to Him one day at a time.

We persevere by continuing in faithfulness to God...Today is the day we focus on.

It's during difficult times that we lean into the love of God to meet us. As the prayer in Ephesians 3:18-21 says, that we "may be able to comprehend with all the saints what is the breadth, and length, and depth, and height; and to know the love of Christ, which passes knowledge, that you might be filled with all the fullness of God." (ESV) He provides friends who will encourage us, providing the same comfort they have received from others.

We are never alone. If we feel misunderstood, or don't know which direction to go next, or if we are sensing we're alone, we can be certain He is right there with us. He does understand our hearts. He does know the next step we need to take.

When we lean into Him and expose our vulnerable hearts to Him, His love speaks loudest. We can dive deep into the scriptures and find truth that meets our needs. When we are at our lowest our spiritual ears seem to be more ready for His voice. Vulnerability before God draws Him. By acknowledging our human weakness, we are open before Him. This is where the strengthening begins. This is precisely where resilience is grown, in His loving Presence.

Resilience in weakness

Our culture ridicules weakness and encourages us to hide or deny our flaws. God's plan for building resilience seems counter-intuitive. As the Apostle Paul wrote, "Therefore, I will boast all the more gladly about my weaknesses, so that Christ's power may rest on me. That is why, for Christ's sake, I delight in weaknesses, in insults, in hardships, in persecutions, in difficulties. For when I am weak, then I am strong." (2 Corinthians 12:9-10, ESV) When we are holding on to God, we are teaching ourselves to not rely on ourselves. We are allowing surrender to be the place we pray from, the attitude we obey from, the way we navigate through crisis.

How do I know the difference? How do I know when I am depending on my own abilities or strengths? One way is to ask, can I do it by myself? Can I make it through this season, this task, this ministry on my own? Or does looking at the road ahead present me with a keen awareness that I cannot under any circumstances go it alone? If it requires faith beyond what I have, then it will require His strength to undertake it and make it through. Trusting Him beyond trusting myself is proof that I'm operating by faith.

We must choose between the mantra-driven, self-exalting kingdom of man, and the scripture-driven, God-exalting kingdom of faith.

Two predominant forces lie in the kingdom of man. Gritting my teeth and pressing through a crisis is known as stoicism. It teaches that becoming more in control of my emotions will allow reason and analytical thinking to develop. Humanism, its sidekick, thrives as man's accomplishments thrive. It sees no need for God. It perpetuates the belief that self-reliance and human ability will solve all problems. It teaches us that I am sufficient in and of myself. I am the boss of me. I control my destiny. We see and hear it touted on every app. It starts with "I can" statements. It is fueled by thoughts that I manifest my own destiny. Humanism claims that by saying "I will" to myself in the mirror, I engage in the mental power to actually form my own future. Those self-reliant voices tell us to mentally power-up to manifest the prosperity that we are entitled to. Of course if I can produce the future, I can produce my identity. Therefore, in this vein, *what I think I can be equals the life I am entitled to.*

In contrast, God's kingdom offers us not self-help, but God's-help. What we know as believers is that we can go the distance and endure all odds in confronting the impossibilities of this life because we are provided for by a God who majors in conquering impossibilities. He provides, guides, and opens doors where previously there was no door. As I take steps of faith led by Him, I am being changed into a likeness of Jesus. Because He is creating life in me, I know I am fully owned and have identity in Him.

What does it mean to be owned by God? It is really about belonging. God has created life throughout the macrocosm of the universe and simultaneously constructs the handiwork in the microcosm of my life. If God sees me as able, forgiven, beautiful, unique, and perfect, then I am the very things He has equipped me with. "...Do not fear, for I have redeemed you; I have summoned you by name; you are mine. When you pass through the waters, I will be with you; and when you pass through the rivers, they will not sweep over you. When you walk through the fire, you will not be burned; the flames will not set you ablaze."(Isaiah 43:1-2)

He will prove to be God of the possible when it looks dark, fruitless and without purpose.

Because I belong to Him, He knows how to configure my way, fulfill His purposes through my life, and forge me into His poetry. "For we are God's handiwork, created in Christ Jesus to do good works, which God prepared in advance for us to do." (Ephesians 2:10)

In my perspective I see Him though through a glass dimly, yet I know Him to be mine. I know this Father God, as the one, true and only God. I am able to see myself through His eyes, as He sees me. I know the precision of His care. He doesn't work haphazardly. He is at work in each circumstance, so I trust Him to change, form and conform my nature to His. These difficult circumstances are His to use as I co-labor with Him.

Self-reliance is not resilience. In fact, the greatest threat to our resilience is our own self-reliance. Taking our eyes off Jesus and focusing on our own resources – or lack of them – will short-circuit our growth and relationship with Him. If we look within ourselves for strength, we begin a long journey into detours that lead to learning the hard way. In time, we will simply be led back around by Him. If we keep looking to Jesus, we will regain the right perspective, course correct and come back to following Him. He will stay on the journey with us. He will keep building resilience as we stay connected through the trials, the hardships, and the impossible circumstances. He will prove to be God of the possible when it looks dark, fruitless and without purpose. If we keep relying on God, we will be able to not only survive but thrive in the challenges that we face. He will feed our resilience with His strength.

An anchor for the soul

Parenting is a marathon. You never stop praying, never stop caring about your child's welfare, wanting the best for them. About a year ago my son's future was weighing heavily on my heart. I was concerned that he was running away from difficult circumstances. He needed a job and some guidance. I asked God to make a way for him, to open doors that would give him hope, and to help me to have peace about it.

That same morning, I was creating art that had nothing to do with my son. Or so I thought. I was creating examples to teach a prayer group to use art to support their prayer life. I began with gluing tissue paper and adding watercolors. The red tissue paper and the blue water-color were intended to be abstract images. But as I added a few thin black Sharpie lines to it, there seemed to be a seascape. The blue represented the sea and the red tissue paper above it became clouds. I drew a fishing boat with an anchor and the little ditty about red skies at night being the sailors' delight came to mind.

The anchor reminded me of the familiar verse in Hebrews 6:19: "We have this hope as an anchor for the soul." God offered me hope even as I created something from nothing. He was telling me that by securing myself to Him, I was safe. The art was providing a means of God turning my focus toward Him instead of my son's hard situation. Through what seemed to be random application of red tissue paper and blue watercolor, He was teaching me to take my focus from the circumstance and put it on Him alone. He was encouraging me to persevere. To have hope.

The next morning my son arrived at our house at 6:30 with exciting news. He was heading north to meet the captain of a fishing ship. He got the name of this captain who needed help from a friend he ran into at the bank. Through a phone call he was hired as a first mate for an albacore fishing boat that was heading out to sea the following week. God was not only answering this mother's prayers about her son's future, He was offering me choices. I could either choose to move forward spiritually with my eyes firmly fixed on Him, or I could remain burdened and anxious about what would happen. Would I let my hope in God be the anchor for my soul and accept His way through these heavy circumstances or would I remain fixed on my own thoughts and solutions? The anchor would hold if I did my part and held onto my hope in Him.

When a crisis strikes, it is easy to feel lost. When panic sets in and circumstances look bleak, finding your way doesn't come easily. You just want to know if it is going to be alright. Will God find you, help you, or rescue you after a fall? Will He make a way for your healing to start and the anxiety to ease? Be reminded of these words from Isaiah 46:4 "...I am He who will sustain you. I have made you and I will sustain you...and I will rescue you." He is promising Himself as your way to the other side of the struggle. He is building resilience in you even as the crisis continues. He will strengthen you when you feel your weakest. But the truth is even when the problems don't have simple or easy solutions, we can create a stable and peaceful space for ourselves. We can change our minds about how we navigate through the problems. We can be changed as we hold onto God despite it all.

God uses the mess

My holding on to God is based on my belief that He is good and what He allows into my life, though not always understood, is for a reason. Kate Bowler, in *No Cure For Being Human*, searingly offers her sentiments as she faced cancer: "It became clearer than ever that life is not a series of choices. So often the experiences that define us are the ones that we didn't pick. Cancer. Betrayal. Miscarriage. Job loss. Mental illness."[3] Even when choices are taken from us, when we have absolutely no control of the circumstances we are facing, we always have the choice to trust Him. I often remind myself when I struggle to understand the difficulties that I am facing, that even if I understand all mysteries, I will still need to trust Him.

God is the origin of goodness. His character is the reason I can securely rest my hope in Him. As Joel Muddamalle eloquently says in his book, *The Hidden Peace*, "The promises of God are rooted in the character of God. God's character is trustworthy and true. If he says he will be with you, you can have confident assurance that he will keep that promise. Why? Because that's just who he is—a promise keeper. And if he is with you, it really doesn't matter who lines up against you, because he who is in you is much greater and more superior than anything this world will try to throw at you."[4] 1 John 4:4 underscores this. "You, dear children, are from God and have overcome them, because the one who is in you is greater than the one who is in the world."

So, we discover that our lives are not about fulfilling the beautiful dream that we had for ourselves. In time we commit to God's plan and a purpose for our lives. He desires that we lay down our lives so He can work in and through us. He had that good plan for us all along: "for it is God who works in you to will and to act in order to fulfill His good pleasure." (Philippians 2: 13)

We sometimes don't see the redemption that He brings through the struggles until the crisis has passed. After some time, I could see God had knitted our young family together in miraculous ways. I asked my grown daughter recently how she felt when I was struggling with cancer. My episodes with cancer were during her pre-school and middle school years and her transition to college just after she graduated from high school. I worried about how it affected my kids. My daughter took a moment to think back to those times and then she said, "Mom, honestly, I did not know how sick you were." I cried. That is proof of His redemption.

Strength for today

I think I would have written this book years ago, except the disease continued. The energy required to heal was formidable. Recurrent cancers can move goals to the back burner. There were long months and then years of harsh therapies, fatigue, and surgeries. I missed events that the family attended without me because of extreme illness and side effects of drugs. I could not work or serve. I could only receive. And that was part of the plan. I would accept help sometimes from unlikely sources. People would show up to make paperwork speed along directing it into the right channels. There was the young pastor working at the Social Security office who ran my disability paperwork through several long steps of administration, assuring that funds would be available. There were nurses, doctors, my pastors, and praying people who showed up on the bleakest days for no other reason than because they were needed. And God knew who to send and when to draw them. The church was a lifeline of prayer, friendship, and counsel. And the meals. We can't overlook the blessing of a dinner in the middle of a disastrous week.

I leaned hard into the arms of our merciful God. I had to trust Him more than I ever had. My life and the hope for my family depended on it. He used those years to grow resilience because I had no other choice. I was between wondering where to hide and wondering if He could keep me hidden. Psalm 139:7 says, "where can I go from your Spirit?" Then Psalm 91:4 contrasts that idea of looking elsewhere with a much better thought: "He will cover you with His feathers, and under his wings you will find refuge..." I opted for the latter. He held onto me when it didn't look like I would make it. He provided rest when I had no strength. What came from one cancer was faith. The next one, grace. The recurrences held hope in Him for a future that I wasn't sure would happen.

A friend recently told me that after those years battling cancer you would think that I would be depleted. But I felt that what had resulted was increased faith. Because those years had stretched over twenty-five, then with the fifth cancer this summer to thirty-four years, I grew a resilient faith that couldn't have happened any other way. Faith was built in the struggle though I couldn't have seen it growing. That certainly doesn't mean it can't be stretched further!

Summer stretch

That stretching and testing came just as I was finishing the manuscript for this book. The cancer returned. It was my second thyroid recurrence; the initial one was twenty-four years prior. Then two recurrences followed. That's right, in the middle of writing a book about resilience I got to see if indeed I could put my words into actions.

I needed to decide: should I put the book on the back burner or gut it out? I am good at taking on challenges, but that lasted about a month. Because of fatigue, I had to stop writing. I was weak, impatient and had a big case of imposter syndrome. In my weakness could I hold onto the hope of finishing the book? Next dilemma: the cancer surgery found more than was expected but the PET scan was inconclusive. Do I focus all my energy on the book, or do I wait?

The answer to that previous question came quickly. I needed to wait until God would tell me to move forward. This is my fifth battle with cancer, I have learned that healing takes time. I decided to wait as my body, mind, and soul were restored. "Go slow!" the Lord had said as I started writing the book several months prior. Now I understand why. He had planned His grace would intervene in the writing schedule. Now He was causing me to give myself that grace. It caused me to pace myself and look for His way in doing it. Realizing that He had made a way from the beginning made the decision to rest easier. Now, I felt that I was moving slower than slow. My efforts in getting back to the desk after the summer of another miracle was more like a turtle than a distance runner. He knew I would need the grace of allowing myself to go slow to heal. I did obey Him, even when everything in me was screaming "Run, Forrest, run!"

There were so many hurdles that kept me from writing that summer. Our family had problems, our business demanded travel. My granddaughter, my joy, was here for the summer, and I was just plain tired. But in my head were quotes, verses about endurance, and books that put my mind on writing for you. What I distilled from those long, hot months: God has a way to build strength in you through your most difficult seasons. His ways are not only best, they are perfect.

Even though I had lived past Stage IV breast cancer twenty years, and even though I have had two thyroid recurrences because I had an anaphylactic response to treatment, I didn't face this one with greater stamina. My hope was in Him to heal me again, that's a given. But my focus was only on getting back up, this time. I was not thinking about what it took to get back up so many other times.

My resilience was not based on my track record. It was the invisible hand of God working many small details together that built my courage and confidence. Yes, He had been there for me in past experiences. I know this. But the strength I needed to go the distance with this cancer was made new by His presence with me in the present battle.

Each time we face a crisis we start fresh in many ways. We have gained a knowledge of His power and strength with each chapter in our lives. But we walk with God in the present. He doesn't change. But our strength must be made new for the present circumstance. We are finite humans. And though we are made for going the distance, we accomplish that distance one step, one day, one episode, one season, one adversity at a time. Truly endurance is not about the ability to handle more, jump higher, or absorb more difficulty. It is not about how far I have come or how far I have to go. It is about the present place of receiving from God today, for the step I take with Him today.

C. S. Lewis has famously said, "God whispers to us in our pleasures, speaks in our conscience, but shouts to us in our pain."[5] Exactly. We need his loving and loud encouragement when facing hard and grievous experiences. And life is full of them. Right? A sudden death, a prodigal child, a misunderstanding that creates distrust, an unfavorable scan result--all shout to us as we navigate through them. But can we hear Him when we are engulfed in pain? As we acknowledge His presence, which is promised to us always, can we tether ourselves to Him even in our doubts? He is with us in pain and suffering. I believe that His love shouts in our pain because in our pain we are aware of our need. Our helplessness is heightened when pain surrounds us. He meets us there. If we let it, painful seasons become opportunities for intimacy with God. Both the pain and the intimacy offer ripe possibilities to experience needed transformation. He uses the difficult season to bring us His good.

The salt and the flower

It was something I'll never forget. My four-year-old daughter, Liz, who was wise beyond her years, wanted to tell me her dream. "Our family was traveling in the van when there was an earthquake." Her bright eyes dazzled as she explained it. "The van shook from side to side so hard that we all lost the pieces of salt we were holding. But Mom, you crawled around on the floor of the van and found everyone's salt and gave it back to them." Then her smile turned somber. "But you couldn't find your own salt. Right then daddy pulled to the side of the road. You opened the door and got out. In front of where you stood, the earth cracked open, and a pink flower grew out of it. You picked the flower and got back in the van."

I had her repeat it over again just so I understood. But I really didn't. They had salt. I found their salt. I got a flower instead. What? I knew that the salt in her dream represented God. Liz didn't know it, but the Bible says God's presence in our lives causes us to flavor and preserve the world. In Matthew 5:13, Jesus said we are "not to lose our savor." Stay salty! God's ownership gives us purpose. Somehow her dream was telling me I would help my family in their holding onto their faith. But what about mine? I didn't have a clue what the flower plucking meant. But I asked Him to show me.

About a year later I read this poem by Carol Trost in Jamie Buckingham's book, *Summer of Miracles*. The poem was sent to him months before he completed that book and only months before his death.

Faith

Faith's blossom is not plucked in pleasant field,
Not so, it grows on craggy height
Where cruel thorns will mend before they yield.
And often the peaceful vale is lost from sight.

Faith does not bloom where placid rivers flow,
'Neath gentle sun, or mild summer shower;
Lo, on storm-blasted mountain see it grow,
And you must brave the storm to pluck the flower.

Yet with what joy your heart will overflow
When you, with bloodied feet, triumphant stand
Upon the summit where faith's flowers grow,
And hold the sacred blossom in your hand.
—Carol Trost[6]

I knew that the Lord was preparing me for what would come. But could I really have known the goodness and kindness that He would wrap me in with every "craggy height" I had to climb? In every season, in every circumstance, His goodness led me, His hand formed me and His love filled me with Himself.

In the same way God is preparing you now. He is allowing you to strengthen your spiritual legs for the climb that will come next. He is providing you with rivers of living water to encourage you on the journey. In Psalm 84:11 it is clear what He offers us. "For the Lord God is a sun and shield; the Lord bestows favor and honor; no good thing does He withhold from those whose walk is blameless." In every kind of weather, He will be your "sun and shield." In every field you must endure, in each mountainous challenge you face, in every threatening storm you are tested by, the Lord will strengthen you, comfort you, and mold you until you "hold the sacred blossom in your hand."

When you walk through the fire

As Tim Keller wrote in his book, *Walking with God through Pain and Suffering*: "In Jesus Christ we see that God actually experiences the pain of the fire as we do. He is truly God with us, in love and understanding, in our anguish. He plunged himself into our furnace so that, when we find ourselves in the fire, we can turn to him and know we will not be consumed but will be made into people great and beautiful."[7]

The spiritual practices in this book have helped you to create a road map for incorporating resilience strategies. These simple practices can renew your mind, and help you develop a strategy to develop and grow from reframing the past. You can alter and fine tune these strategies as the Lord prompts you and dig deeper through the resources mentioned in these pages. You will grow in your ability to gain a new perspective as you rein in hopelessness and get back up from failure. In time, you will see your weaknesses and failed attempts in life as conduits to moving you ahead. You will be building a story that can be shared as He leads you to bring hope and faith to others. Your story will be one that shows how you have persevered. Through the Lord, you have seen resilience built. You now know that what once seemed impossible, is altogether possible.

Our faith in God's goodness builds resilience as we walk through the struggles with Him. We are more than conquerors. We are fueled by His goodness. The difficulties we face are providing deep wells of

God's intimacy and love. We can rely on Him for the strength we lack. He gives us what we need to bend and flex through the hardships that life brings. We can not only endure difficult situations, but we also find purpose and meaning from these experiences. God is working them together to form a resilience that will ground us, support us, and strengthen us. Through our struggles God is forming us into the image and likeness of Jesus.

TAKEAWAYS

- Physically, spiritually, mentally and emotionally we were made for getting back up, again and again and going the distance with the Lord.
- In saying yes to God, we bring the opportunity for miraculous stories to our lives with the choices we make.
- Our greatest threat to our resilience is our own self-reliance. Self-reliance is not resilience.
- We must choose between the mantra-driven, self-exalting kingdom of man, and the scripture-driven, God-exalting kingdom of faith
- When we have absolutely no control of the circumstances we are facing, we always have the choice to trust Him.
- Though we are made for going the distance, we accomplish that distance one step, one day, one episode, one season, one adversity at a time.
- We can change our minds about how we navigate through problems. We are changed as we take steps forward and hold onto God despite it all.
- My endurance is about my present state of receiving from God today, for the step I take with Him today.

Acknowledgments

The people who have supported me as I wrote this book are many. They are lifelong friends and family who have walked with me on this journey.

This book would not have been possible without the support of my husband, Charlie. He challenged me when I thought the road was too long and gave me focus and practical help when I needed it most. As Teddy Roosevelt famously said about those who are willing to push forward in life, he is a true "man in the arena."

Some shared their stories and helped me tell mine with authenticity. Thank you Milissa Little and Mary Pigott! For those who helped me like iron sharpens iron to gear up for writing the hard chapters: Marcia, Megan, Ashley, Milissa, Mickie, and Mary! It paid off in a spiritual battle that I will long remember as victory!

My manuscript readers were also mentors who prayed for me through every step of creating the book. I specifically want to thank: Scott Hilborn, insightful theologian and pastor; Mickie Johnson, my cheerleader, who, along with her husband, Robert, was a persistent prayer supporter; Marcia Braun, my mentor, prayer supporter, and reader; Vicki Harr, mentor and reader; Megan Bielecki, encourager, reader, and literary supporter. I am grateful for you and all you have done.

Those that provided support from inception to completion include Karen Quinn, Karen Heath, Claudia Greco, Ashley Crockett, and Renee Davis. Thank you for always being there, for praying faithfully and for giving whole-heartedly!

Story contributors included friends who wanted to remain anonymous. Your stories supported the beginning of the book and honored me with your time and energy. You are my definition of the body of Christ. You know who you are. Thank you for giving as unto the Lord!

I am grateful that the Lord brought my editor and I together. Keri Wyatt Kent has tirelessly given to make my words shine. Her skill, talent, and sensibilities brought order, structure, and clarity to the book. Early on she had a vision for the book and patiently helped me to see it! Through her work the book will reach many who need its guidance and encouragement!

Recommended Reading

Beholding: Deepening Our Experience in God, Coleman, Strahan, (Colorado Springs, CO.: David C. Cook, 2023)

Building a Resilient Life: How Adversity Awakens Strength, Hope and Meaning, Lyons, Rebekah,(Grand Rapids, Michigan: Zondervan, 2023)

Daring Greatly: How the Courage to be Vulnerable Transforms the Way We Live, Love, Parent and Lead, Brown, Brené, (New York: Avery, 2015)

A Faith that will not Fail: 10 Practices to Build Up Your Faith When Your World is Falling Apart, Cushatt, Michele, (Grand Rapids, Michigan: Zondervan, 2023)

Get Your Life Back: Practices for a World Gone Mad, Eldredge, John, (Nashville: Thomas Nelson, 2021)

The Hidden Peace: Finding True Security, Strength, and Confidence Through Humility, Muddamalle, Joel, (Nashville: W Publishing Group, 2024)

The Hiding Place, ten Boom, Corrie, with John and Elizabeth Sherrill, (New York: Bantam, 1971)

Invitation to Solitude and Silence: Experiencing God's Transforming Presence, Barton, Ruth Haley, (Downers Grove, IL.: InterVarsity Press Books, 2010)

Liturgy of the Ordinary:Sacred Practices in Everyday Life, Warren, Tish Harrison, (Downers Grove, IL.: InterVarsity Press, 2016)

Mindset, The New Psychology of Success, Dweck, Carol, (New York: Ballantine Books, 2007)

No Cure For Being Human: And Other Truths I Need To Hear, Bowler, Kate, (New York: Random House, 2021)

Nothing Wasted: God Uses the Stuff You Wouldn't, Van Norman, Kasey, (Grand Rapids, Michigan: Zondervan, 2019)

Praying Like Monks, Living Like Fools, Staton, Tyler, (Grand Rapids, Michigan: Zondervan, 2022)

Resilient: Restoring Your Weary Soul in these Turbulent Times, Eldredge, John, (Nashville, Thomas Newson, 2022)

The Ruthless Elimination of Hurry, Comer, John Mark, (Colorado: WaterBrook, 2019)

The Sense of the Call, Dawn, Marva, (Grand Rapids, Michigan: Wm. B. Eerdmans Publishing Co., 2006)

The Situation and the Story, Gornick, Vivian, (New York: Farrar, Straus and Giroux, 2001)

Suffer Strong: How to Survive Anything by Redefining Everything, Wolf, Katherine and Jay, (Grand Rapids, Michigan: Zondervan, 2020)

Telling Secrets, Buechner, Frederick, (New York: HarperCollins, 1991)

Walking With God Through Pain and Suffering, Keller, Timothy, (New York: Penguin Group, 2015)

Waiting Isn't a Waste: The Surprising Comfort of Trusting God in the Uncertainties of Life, Vroegop, Mark, (Wheaton, IL.: Crossway, 2024)

Notes

1. GETTING BACK UP

1. Charney, Dennis and Southwick, Steven, *Resilience: The Science of Mastering Life's Greatest Challenges*, (Cambridge: Cambridge University Press, 2018), 45.
2. Helfenbaum, Wendy, "Moving Forward," *Costco Connection*, January, 2024, 29.
3. Sandberg, Sheryl and Grant, Adam, *Option B: Facing Adversity, Building Resilience, and Finding Joy*, (New York: Alfred A. Knopf, 2017).
4. Cushatt, Michele, *I Am* (Grand Rapids, Michigan: Zondervan, 2017), 132.
5. Holmes, Oliver Wendell, "Chambered Nautilus," *One Hundred and One Famous Poems*, (Chicago: The Reilly & Lee Co. Publishers, 1958), 13-14.

2. THINKING OUTSIDE THE BOX

1. Dweck, Carol, *Mindset: The New Psychology of Success* (New York: Ballantine Books, 2007), 53.
2. Tommey, Matt, Matt Tommey Mentoring, "*How to Renew Your Mind: A Simple Guide for Christians*," February 7, 2024, https://mattommeymentoring.com/blog/what-does-the-renewing-if-the-mind-look-like-for-christians.
3. Eldredge, John, *A Prayer for Mental Resilience*, July 31, 2024, https://wildatheart.org/daily-reading/prayer-mental-resilience
4. Barton, Ruth Haley, *Sacred Rhythm: Arranging Our Lives for Spiritual Transformation*, (Downers Grove, Ill.: IVP Books, 2006), 55.

3. WILLING TO WAIT

1. TerKeurst, Lysa, *It's Not Supposed to be this Way: Finding Unexpected Strength When Disappointments Leave You Shattered*, (Nashville: Thomas Nelson, 2018), 45.
2. Wright, N.T., *God-speed, The Pace of Being Known*, https://tinyurl.com/3r3wdnpf
3. Fritz, Sharla, *Waiting: A Bible Study on Patience, Hope, and Trust*, (St. Louis, MO: Concordia, 2017), 21.
4. Marshall, Catherine, *Adventures in Prayer*, (New York: Ballantine, 1975), 60-71.
5. Coleman, Strahan, *Beholding: Deepening Our Experience in God*, (Colorado Springs, CO.: David C. Cook, 2023), 27.
6. Staton, Tyler, *Praying Like Monks, Living Like Fools*, (Grand Rapids, Michigan: Zondervan, 2022), 166.

4. COMBATING CRISIS FATIGUE

1. "*Be Still My Soul*," *The Broadman Hymnal*, (The Broadman Press, Nashville, TN: 1940), 479.

2. Burke, Hilda, quoted in *The Irish Times*, April 11, 2022, Walsh, Geraldine, "Crisis Fatigue Holds Us in a Constant State of Stress."
3. Levine, Harold Dr., Therapist, BayCare Behavioral Health, Blog: "How to Deal with Crisis Fatigue", March 3, 2022, https://baycare.org
4. Warren, Tish Harrison, *Liturgy of the Ordinary: Sacred Practices in Everyday Life*, (Downers Grove, IL: InterVarsity Press, 2016), 35-36.
5. Torrey, R.A., *How To Pray*, (Chicago: Moody Press, 1900), 78.

5. ASKING GOD WHY

1. Nouwen, Henri, *You Turned My Mourning into Dancing: Finding Hope in Hard Times*, (Nashville: Thomas Nelson, 2010), 19.
2. Staton, Tyler, *Praying Like Monks, Living Like Fools*, (Grand Rapids, Michigan: Zondervan, 2022), 57, 58.
3. Sandberg, Sheryl and Grant, Adam, *Option B: Facing Adversity, Building Resilience, and Finding Joy*, (New York: Alfred A. Knopf, 2017), 67-68.
4. Brown, Brené, "The Call to Courage," Director/Editor: Sandra Restrepo, Producers: Dan Efros, Drew Findley, and Jonathan Mussman, 2019. Netflix.cm/title/81010166.
5. McCartney, Paul, and Lennon, John, "The Long and Winding Road," (London: Apple and EMI, 1970).
6. Keller, Timothy, *Walking With God Through Pain and Suffering*, (New York: Penguin Group, 2015), 5.

6. REFRAMING FOR REDEMPTION

1. Beecher, Henry Ward, Attributed to Henry Ward Beecher author, preacher, abolitionist, reformer (1813-1887)
2. Javid, Nazy, August 4, 2018, "Carr Fire Escape: A Redding Dentist Gives Horrific Account of What Happened When She Tried to Escape," Facebook Post featuring KRCR video file. https://tinyurl.com/Dentistescapesfire
3. Gornick, Vivian, *The Situation and the Story*, (New York: Farrar, Straus and Giroux, 2001).
4. Van Norman, Kasey, *Nothing Wasted: God Uses the Stuff You Wouldn't*, (Grand Rapids, Michigan: Zondervan, 2019), 63.
5. Buechner, Frederick, *Telling Secrets,* (New York: HarperCollins, 1991), 33.
6. Van Norman, 30.
7. Ibid, 30

7. FAILING FORWARD

1. ten Boom, Corrie, with John and Elizabeth Sherrill, *The Hiding Place*, (New York: Bantam, 1971), 12.
2. Wolf, Katherine and Jay, *Suffer Strong: How to Survive Anything by Redefining Everything*, (Grand Rapids, Michigan: Zondervan, 2020), 98.
3. Dawn, Marva, *The Sense of the Call*, (Grand Rapids, Michigan: Wm. B. Eerdmans Publishing Co., 2006), 16.

4. Lyons, Rebekah, *Building a Resilient Life: How Adversity Awakens Strength, Hope and Meaning,* (Grand Rapids, Michigan: Zondervan, 2023), 50.
5. Maxwell, John C., *Failing Forward,* (Nashville: Thomas Nelson, 2007), 127.

8. GOING THE DISTANCE

1. Faulkner, Harris, *Faith Still Moves Mountains*, (New York: HarperCollins Publishers, 2022), 168.
2. Ibid, 168.
3. Bowler, Kate, *No Cure For Being Human: And Other Truths I Need To Hear*, (New York: Random House, 2021), 183.
4. Muddamalle, Joel, *The Hidden Peace: Finding True Security, Strength, and Confidence Through Humility,* (Nashville: W Publishing Group, 2024), 22.
5. Lewis, C. S., *The Problem of Pain*, (New York: Harper, 2001), 94.
6. Trost, Carol, "Faith," quoted in Jamie Buckingham's *Summer of Miracles*, (Creation House: Lake Mary, Fla., 1991), 131.
7. Keller, 10.

www.ingramcontent.com/pod-product-compliance
Lightning Source LLC
Chambersburg PA
CBHW071219090426
42736CB00014B/2892